CANOEING

CANOEING

The Complete Guide to Equipment and Technique

DAVE HARRISON

STACKPOLE BOOKS

Published in 1996 by
STACKPOLE BOOKS
5067 Ritter Road
Mechanicsburg, PA 17055

Published by arrangement with Sports Illustrated Books, a division of Time Inc.

Printed in the United States of America

Cover photograph by Scott Spiker
Cover design by Tina M. Hill

Photo credits: Marlin Bayes/Western Canoeing: pages 13, 50 (bottom); courtesy *Canoe & Kayak* magazine: pages 76, 109 (bottom), 116, 120, 172; Dave Harrison: pages 10, 12, 14, 15, 16, 19, 21, 36, 39, 43, 44, 46, 48, 50 (top), 56, 57, 60, 61, 68, 88, 91, 105 (bottom), 117 (bottom), 122, 125, 128, 133, 136, 138, 140, 154, 155, 159, 161, 164, 169, 170, 178, 180, 182, 185, 189; courtesy of Lotus Canoe: page 120 (bottom); The Mariners Museum, Newport News, VA: page 18 (top); The Public Archives of Canada: page 18 (bottom); Slim Ray: pages 111, 113; R. Hamilton Smith: page 117 (top); Will Summer/*Canoe & Kayak* magazine: page 175; George Thomas: page 106; all other photographs by Tom Ettinger.

Diagrams and illustrations by H. Russel Suiter and David Besenger.

The map on page 141 was drawn by Stephen Gussman and appears in *New England White Water Guide* by Ray Gabler, copyright © 1975 by Ray Gabler.

First Stackpole edition

10   9   8   7   6   5   4   3   2   1

Library of Congress Cataloging-in-Publication Data

Harrison, David, 1938–
    [Sports illustrated canoeing]
    Canoeing : the complete guide to equipment and technique/ Dave Harrison.
       p. cm.
    Originally published as: Sports illustrated canoeing. New York :
Sports illustrated, © 1988.
    ISBN 0-8117-2426-3 (pbk.)
      1. Canoes and canoeing.   I. Title.
GV783.H38 1996
797.1'22—dc20   95-44934
                                           CIP

Contents

Acknowledgments

This is a book about canoes and canoeing, the product of my lifelong love affair with a craft that is a genuine North American invention. Kayaks, rafts, dories, and rowing boats can duplicate some of the functions of the canoe, but none possesses the canoe's versatility. In form, only the kayak could be considered a sibling.

Sharing my love of canoes and canoeing is my wife, Judy, who patiently assisted in researching and organizing the material for this book. To Lee and Judy Moyer, proprietors of Pacific Water Sports in Seattle, who provided both expert advice and equipment, and to Ulrich and Nono, and to Steve, paddlers extraordinaire, we extend our thanks for their support.

Introduction

From the Arboretum to the Arctic

I have the good fortune to live in Seattle, a city perhaps more abundantly blessed than most with both natural and manmade refuges for recreation. From the windows of my commuter bus, during four or five months of the year, I can see couples paddling among the serpentine channels of the University of Washington Arboretum. Several channels extend under the freeway, whose columnar supports create a surrealistic slalom course. Not far away, in fact, suspended between two diverging branches of the freeway, is a complete set of actual slalom gates, a practice course for canoers and kayakers from the university.

Beyond the protected channels of the arboretum and the security of its concrete wilderness lies a lake, where, thanks to farsighted city planners, forty-foot powerboats, sailboats large and small, wind surfers, hydroplanes, and canoes coexist on pleasant, unpolluted waters. Into this larger world venture forth those canoers who have advanced beyond the hesitant strokes of the more timid paddlers in the arboretum. They catch my eye. Surely, the same confidence and curiosity that lures them onto the broad expanses of the lake is a giant step toward further exploration by canoe. While greater mastery and broader horizons are

11

Canoers returning from an evening paddle on a lake in Maine.

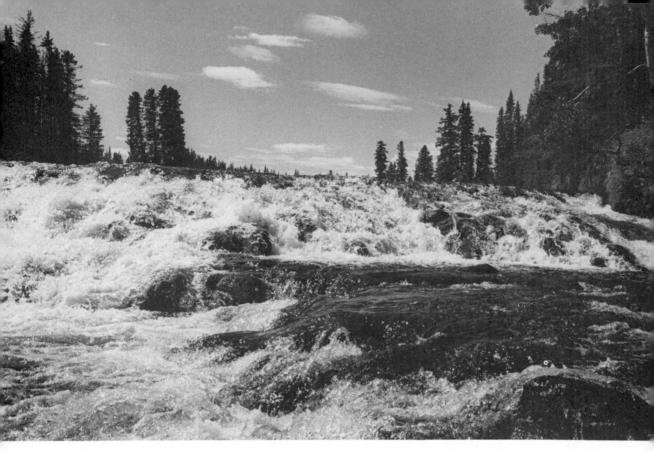

More remote environments will lure the experienced canoeist.

worthy goals in any sport, there is equal value in the pleasures and relaxation enjoyed by those who go no farther than the lily pads marking the outer boundaries of the arboretum.

Perhaps the canoe's greatest virtue is that it makes larger a world which in most other ways is becoming ever smaller. Inquisitive canoers can spend an entire afternoon of exploration and discovery in the arboretum, which my rush-hour bus races past in a few moments. A continent away, in New Jersey, the most densely populated state in the nation, one can canoe for hours in the relative solitude of the Great Swamp or the Pine Barrens. I once spent seven hours there, winding my way down one of the piney rivers with a family group and seeing only one other person—a kayaker. Well, that's not quite true. One mile from our destination we passed under a wooden footbridge and were greeted from overhead by some walkers, who asked where the river went. "To the ocean" was our simple reply.

All rivers share this common destiny. And both the river bound for the Arctic Ocean after a trip of a thousand miles and the one that meanders toward the Atlantic through the pine barrens in the shadow of metropolis are suitable for enjoyment and exploration. Adventure is where you find it, and only time and appetite should limit the extent of one's journeys. I am as fascinated by the bird- and wildlife inhabiting a suburban slough as by the lush, dripping canopy of an Olympic Peninsula rain-forest river, or the foaming cataracts of a remote and seldom-traveled wild river in northern Canada.

Urban adventures are possible as well. In the United States, as in Europe, canals and waterways still exist whose commercial use is long since over but whose populated banks tell you a hundred stories. City parks, arboretums, or lakes surrounded by houses and condominiums also invite exploration. There is something appealing about canoeing that usually brings forth a friendly response from those into whose territory you might stray.

There are no age barriers in canoeing. Young and old alike can share its many pleasures.

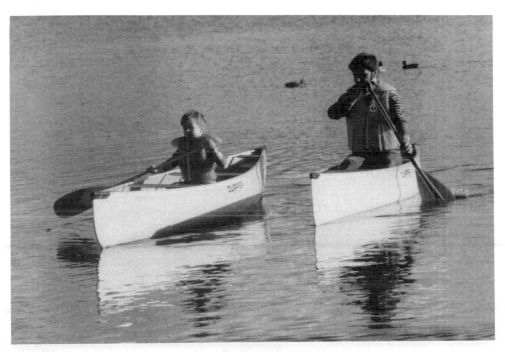

Canoeing can be an end in itself: a Sunday paddle, a picnic, two hours' escape. Or it may be strictly for exercise. It is a more serious activity for canoers who graduate to the world of white water, pitting themselves each weekend against precipitous rivers, or for those who thrive on competition and enter the varied events of competitive canoeing—marathons, wild water, slaloms, or even poling. For many, the ultimate is the canoe trip or expedition, conjuring up nostalgic visions of Indians and early explorers.

Canoeing is both an activity in itself and a means to the enjoyment of other pursuits. Because it glides unobtrusively into places accessible in few other ways, the canoe is often the vehicle of choice for photographers, fishermen, artists, geologists, birdwatchers, historians, and prospectors. The canoe becomes your magic carpet to remote nooks and crannies, as you will find yourself becoming photographer, fisherman, geologist, ornithologist, and historian as well.

The chapters that follow will introduce you to the canoe, and the skills it requires, before going on to explore some of the possibilities and frontiers of canoeing, so that you may follow your own vision of the sport, whether your destination be the arboretum or the arctic.

Birdwatching and wildlife sighting may be your reason for canoeing, but for the young people above the canoe is the perfect craft for fishing.

1

A Boat for Every Occasion

Like the wheel, the canoe of the Algonquin Indian has been improved only slightly by technology, and those improvements have been in the materials used rather than in hull forms or principles. No other craft, except possibly the Eskimo kayak, combines so well the elements of speed, maneuverability, lightness, and load-carrying capacity. The dugouts of the Kootenay Indians were magnificent boats that made the best use of available materials, the huge trees in the forests of the Pacific Northwest, but they lacked the flexibility of design to become all-purpose craft. The flat-bottomed pirogue of the Louisiana bayous looks like a poor man's canoe, but simplicity of construction from available materials to serve fishermen on still waters justifies its existence.

Early North American Watercraft

The predecessor of the modern canoe could only have been invented in the northern forests, where the gums, natural sinews, and, critically, the canoe birch stood ready to provide the materials for a boat that could be built on the spot without a single nail. It is remarkable that ribs steamed to shape along a keelson, set in a form of wooden

17

Wood and canvas, the canoer's equivalent of Chippendale.

Malecite canoe.

stakes, planked longitudinally, and covered with birch bark could so effectively merge attributes of hull speed, strength, weight, and displacement in a design that would survive through the centuries.

In the eighteenth and nineteenth centuries, the canoe achieved its penultimate form in the Montreal and North canoes, which bore the loads of explorers and voyagers who, in their pursuit of the fur trade and other commerce, drew the map of Canada and found their way to the Pacific and Arctic oceans. The mighty Montreal canoes, 35 to 40 feet in length, carried a crew of fourteen and were capable of holding loads of almost three tons. These *canots de maîtres* were used on larger bodies of water, such as the Great Lakes and the St. Lawrence River. At Grand Portage on the western shore of Lake Superior their cargo of supplies bound for the interior posts was exchanged for furs brought in smaller North canoes by brigades from the interior of Canada.

Canot de maître, or Montreal canoe, shooting the rapids.

Despite their size, the formidable loads, and the rugged routes they traveled, these workhorses of the fur trade were fragile craft, held together by threads of watape, especially the root of the red spruce. The bark covering was made watertight through gumming with pine pitch, a repair that had to be undertaken frequently, en route. The journals of early fur traders such as Peter Pond, David Thompson, and Alexander Mackenzie make constant reference to this discouraging interruption. Mackenzie, in his successful westward journey to the Pacific Ocean, was forced to abandon his torn and waterlogged canoes at the Fraser River in British Columbia and finish the journey overland.

The Modern Canoe

About one hundred years ago, the direct descendant of the Indian birchbark canoe and forerunner of the modern lightweight canoe was crafted in Canton, New York, by J. Henry Rushton, whose classic Nessmuk model was 10½ feet long and 27 inches wide and weighed only 18½ pounds. This cedar boat was of lapstrake construction, the planking individually planed and butted to be completely watertight. In his later canoes, Rushton incorporated some economical design features, which others had begun to develop by stretching a canvas covering over a hull of wooden ribs and planking. The watertight integrity of the newer craft was the result of technology rather than the painstaking craftsmanship required in the all-wood canoe.

The traditional wood and canvas canoe is the product of painstaking hand labor.

In 1902 the Old Town Canoe Company was incorporated, and to this day their wood and canvas canoes (more recently, the canvas has been replaced by fiberglass) set a high standard of workmanship. Ironically, this construction, which superseded the prohibitively expensive all-cedar construction of the early Rushtons, seemed for a time to be itself threatened, not through any deficiencies of performance or change in hull design, but by economics. But wood is back. Today, Old Town is not alone. A recent survey of canoe manufacturers revealed over 100 builders of wooden canoes, albeit many in the custom category.

CANOE DESIGNS

Before worrying about materials, let's look at today's hull shapes and purposes. Start with the logical assumption that a wide, flat-bottomed canoe, with the width carried well into the ends, will be slow but initially stable, while a long needle-nosed hull with a deep, narrow cross section (deep V'd) is going to be fast, hard to turn, and unstable (at least in the hands of an inexperienced paddler).

Stability and Maneuverability

The question of design becomes more complicated when you discover that this flat-bottomed canoe, while stable in quiet waters, may become quite unstable in heavy seas or white water. It may also be a revelation to learn that a longer greater-volume boat will handle more easily than a shorter small-capacity boat. A 15-foot canoe is *not* easier to handle than a 17-foot canoe. Once you put two people and 150 pounds of gear into the smaller canoe, the increased load causes it to sink farther into the water. Now you have to move the canoe against a greater volume of water, producing the same kind of friction that slows the forward momentum of a wide, flat-bottomed canoe.

Length

Most recreational canoes for two paddlers will be 15 to 18 feet in length. This is true whether they are used for canoe tripping, white water, or pleasure cruising. Solo paddlers will prefer the lower end of this range, unless they are out for speed (see Chapter 7). Personal or "pack" boats for the solo paddler might be 14 feet or less. For two paddlers, there are few applications for which a 17-foot canoe is not suitable. Therefore, add or subtract 6 to 18 inches, depending on the uses and loads to which the boat will be subjected. Canoes in excess of 18 feet are often the choice of expeditioners to provide comfortable load-carrying capacity. Whether loaded or not, there are other factors to be considered by the performance minded. Other things being equal, a long canoe will be faster than a short canoe because canoes are governed by the physics of *displacement* hulls. That means that speed will equal 1.55 times the square root of the waterline length. Thus the maximum or potential speed (displacement speed) of an 18½-foot canoe is 6.7 miles per hour; a 15-footer, 6.0 miles per hour.

Keel vs. Keel Line

A boat with a high rocker bottom—one with a pronounced curve from end to end, like a chair rocker—will turn quickly, whereas a long straight keel line—whether the boat has an actual keel or not (and increasingly they do not)—is designed for speed rather than maneuverability. Keel "line" describes the rocker or presence or absence of a V, and it is these design characteristics that affect a canoe's quick-turning and tracking properties (the canoe's tendency to glide in a straight line). A keel may provide some degree of protection, or be a part of a canoe's structural integrity, but in the absence of other hull characteristics, its contribution to tracking capability is slight. And in white water or fast-moving rivers a keel is a downright liability.

This high rocker boat is designed for fast turning.

Canoe hulls (from left to right, aluminum, ABS, fiberglass, and wood) reflect a variety of requirements as well as the design limitations of the material.

Only the aluminum canoe (rear) has a keel. Of these recreational canoes, the extended keel line of the fiberglass (second from foreground) suggests a faster hull.

Round, flat, and "V"-bottomed hulls.

The endless ingenuity of designers and manufacturers in blending different cross sections, bow curvatures, and keel lines has created a variety of hulls for every conceivable use or combination of uses. The pictures provide only a sampling. Simply combining two or three elements fails to tell the whole story, since factors such as length, width at the gunwale (the upper edge of the canoe's side), width at the four-inch waterline (an arbitrary point of measurement to determine tumblehome—described below), depth, and, more importantly, how far into the bow and stern certain of these elements are carried, must also be considered. As an extreme example, a deep-V hull (normally associated with fast boats) used with a snub-nosed bow and stern would be about as fast as a hollow log.

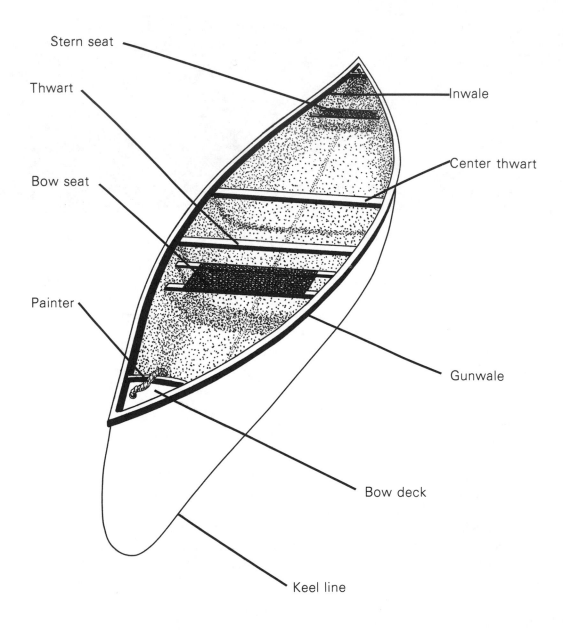

Stern seat

Thwart

Bow seat

Painter

Inwale

Center thwart

Gunwale

Bow deck

Keel line

Capacity

How much a boat holds obviously depends on length, but depth at center, width, and fullness at the waterline (sometimes referred to as "tumblehome") also affect capacity. Since a common standard is lacking, you should consult your dealer for capacities of specific boats. A well-designed recreational canoe suitable for a wide range of cruising, canoe tripping, or white water should hold between 650 and 1,000 pounds of paddlers and baggage. There should be at least 6 inches of the canoe's side showing between the level of the water and the upper edge of the boat when it is fully loaded. This is known as the freeboard. Less than 6 inches of freeboard is unsafe.

What to Avoid

Perhaps the best way to learn about design is to discuss the features you *don't* need until you reach a point, or use, where a certain design element will make an important difference in your canoe's performance (such as for heavy white water, slalom or flat-water racing, or solo paddling).

First, avoid the extremes, whether they are flat-bottomed, round or deep V'd, or highly rockered. A long keel line combined with a V hull is OK for cruising, but avoid it if you plan to paddle in winding rivers or even moderate rapids.

Generally speaking, for two paddlers avoid canoes of less than 16 feet in length or greater than 18½ feet; canoes with less than 34 inches or more than 37 inches of width at the gunwale line amidships; or less than 13 inches in depth; that is, unless you plan to canoe solo or have performance canoeing in mind (which we'll get into in Chapter 7).

Avoid canoes that weigh too much—over 80 pounds. (There has never been a canoe that weighed too little!) And, finally, don't go for the lowest-priced canoe. With its versatility and long life, a canoe costing $1,500 is a bargain when compared to most other watercraft—or, in fact, to most recreational equipment.

CANOE MATERIALS

As the number of canoers grows each year, so does the impetus to develop advanced designs and new materials to meet their increasingly sophisticated requirements. Currently there are half a dozen different materials used for canoe hulls: wood, aluminum, fiberglass, Kevlar 49, and various other plastics.

Wood

The case for wood canoes can be made on entirely aesthetic grounds, for they are objects of beauty and warmth. Sufficient hull designs exist in wood to meet all but the most specialized uses, and the modern wood canoe's durability has been enhanced by combining it with other materials, including fiberglass, resin oil, and improved canvas fillers, so that a well-constructed wood canoe has strength-to-weight characteristics that compare very favorably to some of the newer materials.

Originally, lead was used as a component in the canvas fillers of wood and canvas canoes. Later, to comply with health regulations, some manufacturers substituted fiberglass for canvas. The fiberglass, however, gave the canoe a harder feel, not the creaking, soft feel that many of us had come to love. Fortunately, nonlead canvas fillers have been developed, making it possible to buy safe canoes with that desirable soft feel. These canoes are resilient and easy to repair.

If you should have a chance to lay your hands on an old-style wood and canvas canoe, it will, if properly cared for, last a lifetime. The wood canoe does not stand up to mishandling and reckless technique, and of course it requires more maintenance than the newer models. Nevertheless, having paid a premium for the canoer's equivalent of the Chippendale, the owner of a wood canoe should find its maintenance a labor of love.

Aesthetics alone could make the premium-priced wood-strip canoe your choice.

Aluminum

Thirty years ago aluminum canoes were the leading seller, and there is still a huge population in active use. Their popularity has waned considerably with the introduction of new materials and designs. They are durable, lightweight, and inexpensive, and their standard designs provide for a wide range of recreational uses. Produced in volume with a limited number of hull shapes, aluminum canoes were created for mass-market use and have been for many years the staple of outfitters and canoe liveries. Aluminum is definitely a material that merits the canoe buyer's serious consideration.

All aluminum canoes are not created equal, and construction methods, quality of temper, thickness of the aluminum skin, and hull shapes differ from manufacturer to manufacturer. Price—you tend to get what you pay for—and manufacturer's reputation are probably your most reliable guides.

No canoe is indestructible, but the best aluminum canoes come close. Without question, they are the most carefree. Because of the hull-forming and riveting processes in aluminum canoe manufacture, there are definite limitations in design. But the most popular 17- and 18-footers represent only a modest performance compromise, when the factors of durability, utility, weight, and price are considered.

Some people complain that the aluminum canoe is too cold or too hot, and too noisy, and that it sticks to rocks. To others, aluminum is just plain unappealing. However, if utility and longevity are more important to you than appearance and feel, go for aluminum.

Fiberglass

A good fiberglass canoe will compete favorably in price with other synthetics and with wood, and, depending on the design and manufacturing method, provide very satisfactory weight-to-strength characteristics.

A "good" fiberglass canoe, however, is dependent on many factors, the most important being the quality and method of "lay-up." This refers to the number of layers of fiberglass cloth used in its construction. In general, more layers are better. There are as many varieties of lay-ups, resins, and molding and curing techniques as there are manufacturers, including the innovative craftsman who turns out a canoe a week in his garage. A good fiberglass canoe is not a mass-produced item but represents many hours of hand labor. The mold can embody the most exacting refinements of the canoe builder's art to achieve the optimum performance for that canoe's intended use.

There are a number of fiberglass boats on the market which are abominations—too heavy, crude of design—cheap "chopper gun" concoctions. Hand-laid-up fiberglass boats will generally be of higher quality.

The buyer of a fiberglass canoe must exercise much greater care and put a good deal more faith in the dealer or manufacturer than when buying a canoe of any other material. Since the subject of fiberglass construction is reasonably complicated, you would be well advised to shop for a fiberglass boat—in fact, any canoe—at stores specializing in canoes, as opposed to sporting goods stores carrying everything from fishing tackle to bowling balls. You should also ask experienced canoeing friends or folks in your local kayak and canoe club for guidance. If you do not go for a major brand name, these people are likely to have strong opinions about some of the smaller producers who may be turning out boats for your local or regional market.

Super Fabrics

Today the best known super fiber for canoes is Kevlar 49, a Du Pont aramid fiber similar to fiberglass, but with greater tensile strength, and greater resistance to tearing and abrasion. Like fiberglass, Kevlar is laid up in a mold and impregnated with resin, and usually finished off with a smooth outer layer called the gel coat. Other tough fabrics include S-glass, hybrid weaves of glass and polyester, Kevlar layered with fiberglass, and combos stiffened or supplemented with graphite and foam. The latest entrant in the fabric derby is Spectra 900, from Allied Chemical.

The results are boats of incredible strength and light weight. A high volume tripping boat can be produced in one of the proprietary (hybird) lay-ups weighing 60 pounds, in Kevlar 49 at a mere 50 pounds, and with foam and a bit of graphite, less still. Prototype race boats made with Spectra 900 are the lightest and strongest yet produced. But these super fibers are expensive and hard to work with; like top-end bicycles, the price of the boat rises exponentially with the decline in weight. For the racer and the paddler looking for motion pleasure and the highest return on his energy investment, that's a price worth paying.

ABS Royalex

Royalex is Uniroyal's name for a multilaminated sandwich of vinyl and ABS—acrylonite-butadiene-styrene—with a closed-cell foam core. Old Town calls it Oltonar. Other canoe manufacturers use either the Royalex name or their own;

while the hull-forming process may be proprietary to a particular manufacturer, they use basically the same material.

What's unique about ABS Royalex? The molecularly cross-linked vinyl provides a durable surface, the ABS offers penetration resistance, and the foam gives backbone (plus flotation) to an otherwise sloppy laminate. These features produce considerably more durability than fiberglass, while not being as expensive as Kevlar. In addition, the foam core in the laminate gives the material its own flotation—as opposed to aluminum or fiberglass, where flotation must be built in or provided. (Wood, of course, also provides its own natural flotation.)

Those are the good qualities of ABS Royalex, but for the purist the thickness of the laminate means a weight penalty and limitations on the sharpness of line. You just cannot get the same fine, cut-through-the-water bow in ABS Royalex that you can in fiberglass or Kevlar. Nevertheless, it appears to be the material most directly competitive to aluminum in providing good all-round recreational hulls that are virtually indestructible and reasonably priced.

Polyethylene

Several years ago, a leading manufacturer of camping equipment introduced a thermo-formed, high density polyethylene craft and called the material Ram-X. Inexpensive and virtually indestructible, the craft became the best-selling canoe in America. Recently, another manufacturer found a way to fabricate a rigid polyethylene canoe, which eliminated the need for the awkward internal frame in the pioneer designs, resulting in a much more aesthetic and functional craft. Poly canoes are still on the heavy side, but price and indestructability make them worthy of serious consideration.

THE RIGHT BOAT

Earlier in the chapter we talked about what to avoid in selecting a canoe. Now it is time to inject *you* into the equation. Consider that every material or design represents some kind of compromise or trade-off. However, where you live, how you vacation, how often you expect to canoe, and the type of available water inevitably will point toward the most suitable craft for you. A family canoe is going to be a different boat from the one with which you expect to do some serious racing, and yet there are a number of designs that are just as appropriate for canoe tripping with the kids as for use in white water.

The canoe design and material that meets your highest and most likely use is the right choice. For people living in Illinois, it would make little sense to purchase a boat with a high rocker and white-water capabilities if they are only planning to use their canoe locally, just as it would be a waste of money to buy a Wonacott, cedar-strip canoe, or Jensen racer to keep tied to your dock on Half-Acre Pond. For the serious paddling family it's not unusual to find half a dozen or more canoes (plus a kayak, or two) to meet a variety of needs, from fishing to fast cruising to expedition work or family canoe tripping.

Suitability Table

There is no canoe built that cannot be put to some use for which it was not designed, and fortunately there is enough overlap in design and materials capability to enable one canoe to meet a number of requirements. The table opposite takes a stab at correlating materials, designs, and use; however, it is one man's perception, and there will be exceptions in every case. Aluminum-canoe enthusiasts may insist, for example, that there are special races *just* for aluminum canoes and argue that they are the only white-water boat; so be it.

The absence of a check mark in some cases does not indicate unsuitability, only that I would have other preferences.

Shop for Value

One more thought on price and its corollaries: Unless your canoe is destined for only the most occasional use, buy the best canoe you can afford. Yet be conscious of design and canoer acceptance. There is always room for individuality, but owning a canoe with an oddball shape or tacky workmanship will detract from your full enjoyment of this sport.

If you try to buy a good used canoe, you will discover that they hardly exist. By the same measure, your well-chosen canoe of good manufacture should never depreciate in value if reasonably maintained.

CARING FOR THE CANOE

Fortunately, most canoes require little or no care, the exception being the wood canoe, which you buy with the thought that you will revel in its care and

The absence of a check mark in some cases does not indicate unsuitability, only that I would have other preferences.

	Pleasure	Family	Canoe Tripping	White Water	Flat-water Racing**	White-water Racing	Utility (camp or group use)
Aluminum	x	x	x				x
Wood	x	x	x		x		
Fiberglass	x	x	x		x		
Kevlar		x	x	x	x	x	
ABS or Poly	x	x	x	x		x	x
Flat bottom	x	x	x				x
Round bottom				x		x	
Deep V					x		
Shallow V	x	x	x	x	x		
Straight keel	x	x	x		x		x
Moderate rocker		x	x	x		x	x
High rocker				x		x	
Under 75 pounds*	x	x	x	x	x	x	x
Over 75 pounds	x			x			x

*There was never a canoe that was too light, but you may not wish to pay the premium for a lightweight boat if your intended use is occasional or utilitarian.

**Also fast touring. See chapter 7 and discussion of performance canoes, including extreme lightweight boats, with minimal waterline widths, and asymmetrical hulls.

maintenance. I can think of no piece of recreational equipment that is so forgiving of neglect and whose performance is so unaffected. (Imagine, if you will, the ten-speed bicycle whose derailleur or chain goes uncleaned or unoiled for two years.) This is not an invitation to sloppiness. A sense of tidiness and pride of ownership will usually motivate canoers to clean the sand and grit from inside their boats, massage the abrasions on their fiberglass boats with acetone, or wax the hulls of their aluminum canoes. But unless a boat must be kept to some performance standard for racing, or unless forward motion, comfort, or portaging weight are affected, maintenance is more a matter of choice than necessity.

Canoes, regardless of material, tend to sustain more injuries on dry land or within three feet of shore than in all the white water in the Americas, usually as a result of being dropped, dragged, rammed, or tramped in while sitting on land. My canoe trips have taken me and my boats into some of the ruggedest canoeing environments on earth, but disabling accidents have been few and far between, and most of the injuries sustained have required no more than a piece of duct tape to repair. Remember that the first canoes were constructed in the forest. Seats, thwarts, gunwales, and decks can all be fashioned out of local materials, if need be.

Duct tape makes a good temporary patch. Just be sure the hull surface is dry before applying.

Wood

Wood and wood-canvas canoes obviously require a good deal more attention than other boats, but they are a lot more resilient than most people realize. The former Chestnut Canoe Company in Canada told of a canoe owned by a Mr. Kennedy, the first member of Parliament from the Yukon Territory, who in 1963 contacted the Chestnut factory to ask if they would canvas and refurbish his 16-foot Prospector—used on the Yukon during the Klondike Gold Rush of 1898 and in steady use ever since.

If you are going to own a wood canoe, your loving care for it will be directly proportional to the premium you paid and your recognition that this object of beauty requires more than a kick in the ribs from time to time. Fortunately, many of the newer wood canoes have been treated or fiberglassed to be more resistant to moisture, puncture, and cracking than the earlier wood and wood-canvas models. To the extent that wood is exposed, because of age or injury, its principal enemies are sand and grit and moisture. The first two act as abrasives and will add weight by working their way into the cracks and the wood grain itself. Moisture also adds weight and, over time, may lead to rot.

At a minimum, wood canoes should be hosed out periodically, or swamped in lake or river to flush out the sand and grit. A sponge can finish off the job and get out the excess moisture. During the off season, a light sanding followed by a coat of marine varnish will prolong the life of the wood surfaces. If you sand the old coat carefully, you will minimize additions to the boat's weight. Less frequently, canvas will have to be sanded down and a new coat of paint applied, preferably sprayed on. Torn canvas is easily repaired, using a fiberglass patch. I have effected semi-permanent patches, under way, by cutting a patch out of a bandanna, slipping it in between the canvas and the wood planking, and filling in the torn area with airplane cement. Later, a couple of licks of paint on top made the patch almost unnoticeable.

Other Repairs and Maintenance

The most vulnerable areas of a canoe tend to be in its underbelly, just ahead of the stern and just behind the bow. On rocks and under heavy use, even the toughest materials begin to wear thin here. Aluminum is probably the least affected. As ABS Royalex has gradually made inroads with the livery and outfitting people, they have found it necessary to epoxy Kevlar "bang plates"

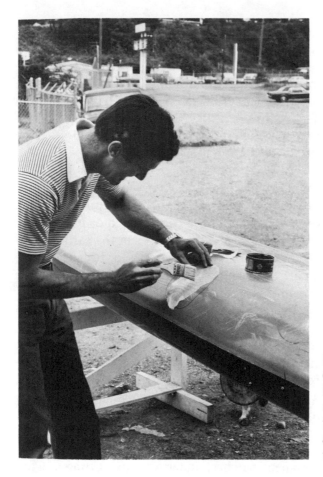

Resin, catalyst, fiberglass cloth, and a cheap paint brush are all you need to make a permanent repair to a fiberglass canoe. All are available in hardware and automotive stores.

to the vulnerable bow and stern areas in order to extend their canoes' life. You can do the same. Or, if you are not a stickler for looks, applying multiple layers of duct tape to these areas will help.

Having patched your canoe's injuries with duct tape while on the river, you will eventually tire of looking at them and decide to put on a more permanent patch. Most hardware, automotive, or marine stores carry fiberglass cloth and cans of resin (with their companion catalyst) and, except for the mind-warping smell, it is an easy matter to follow the directions on the can and make a permanent patch. You will need a piece of cloth, a coffee can in which to mix resin and catalyst, a cheap paintbrush (it will have to be thrown away after one use), and sandpaper to clean and roughen the area to be patched. A temperature in the seventies and good ventilation are important. Kevlar canoes can be patched with fiberglass, or you can obtain special patching materials from your dealer.

Putting a hole in an aluminum or ABS canoe is a feat in itself, and duct tape will suffice for temporary repairs on these as well. Permanent repairs require more specialized attention than can be covered here. That's the time to call the dealer.

If your aluminum canoe sustains a major or minor dent, a good semblance of the original shape can be recouped with a well-placed kick to the damaged area, or, if more precision is called for, a few adroitly placed strokes with a rubber mallet or a sock filled with sand. The same is true of ABS Royalex, which also responds well if warmed. In fact, ABS has some "memory," and a major dimple received on the river in the morning may well pop out after your canoe sits tied on top of your car in the sun for fifteen minutes.

Polyethylene boats present some interesting problems, because we now have two types: linear and cross-linked. The former are less rigid and can be treated by a good canoe doctor using high heat. However, at present, there is no generally available method for repair of cross-linked poly boats; still, they can take nearly the equivalent of a direct torpedo hit and bounce back. It's likely to be the seats, decks or gunwales in these dreadnoughts that need repair in the event of a shelling.

2

Paddles, PFDs, and Appurtenances

Having chosen your canoe, you have made your toughest decision and perhaps a compromise, as well. Choosing paddles is much easier and there is plenty of room for experimentation. Other accessories for the canoer involve minimal cost or are easily improvised.

PADDLES

A paddle is a simple device. Those used by the Indians in their dugouts and canoes were nothing more than wooden poles with one end hewn to some semblance of flatness. Up to a few years ago, most paddles for recreational purposes were made of ash, spruce, or maple, and, except for regional eccentricities of blade shape, they were only a modest improvement over the native originals. If you can still find one of these in a good straight-grained wood, they make fine all-purpose paddles, but avoid the "popsicle sticks" sold in sporting goods and boat stores—usually stacked in a barrel and meant to be emergency tools for motorboaters.

The paddle does represent an extension, in every sense of the word, of you, the paddler. Let

Many paddlers prefer the feel of a wood paddle. The bent-shaft paddles, originally developed for racing, are increasingly popular for recreational cruising, even tripping.

37

your paddle selection be an ego trip, if you will, but remember this: Any paddle of good quality will do the job.

Wood Paddles

Today, synthetics have largely replaced the one-piece ash or spruce paddle, but you can satisfy your aesthetic cravings with one of the handsome laminated wooden paddles on the market. A good laminated paddle is lightweight, strong, and warm and has a spring—or flex—that many paddlers find pleasing, especially over long distances. Costing $20 to $30, and laminated from selected woods, they can weigh as little as 1 or 2 pounds. To compensate for a thin profile or the use of lighter, softer wood, more laminations or a single layer of clear fiberglassing and a metal or fiberglass tip are added for reinforcement. The grips are of two types, the pear and the T. The former is generally used for cruising and the latter for racing and white water.

Synthetics

As you might suspect, the durability and variety of the synthetics makes them increasingly popular. Unfortunately, some are popular because of low price and are even cruder implements than the Indian originals. One should be prepared to pay $25 or more for a good synthetic paddle. It will have a blade of epoxy, fiberglass, or Kevlar, with a tempered, round, or oval aluminum shaft, covered

White-water paddlers prefer a T grip, but for most paddling, the shape of the grip makes little difference.

Synthetic paddles come in a variety of shapes, weights, and sizes. Durability might be one good reason for choosing a synthetic. The bent shaft paddles pictured here weigh only 14 to 16 ounces.

with plastic to minimize the conductivity of heat and cold. My own preference is for a polyester or fiberglass shaft (hollow, like a fishing rod) that has some flex—that is, the feel of wood—and with a blade that is durable and yet as thin as possible. There are some epoxy blades that will withstand the roughest white water or canoe-tripping treatment without a tip protector; other blade materials need this protection. For most synthetics, T grips seem to be the overwhelming favorite, but now the variations on the T are so numerous that only your hand will be able to make the decision. Again, the T grip is usually the choice of whitewater paddlers because it increases blade control.

Other Designs and Materials

More exotic designs are available to the specialized user or the equipment freak; the bent-shaft paddles originally designed for marathon and flat-water racing are one such example. Usually made of fine laminated woods, many such paddles today are made of synthetics and weigh in at less than 20 oz. While expensive, they are promoted by some enthusiasts as being easier to use, providing a greater forward reach and a smoother, faster stroke while reducing the porpoising (bobbing) tendency of a canoe under a full head of steam.

New paddles, aimed primarily at the racing and performance cruising market, are now coming in at an amazing 14 to 20 ounces. They are usually bent shaft with varying combinations of Kevlar, graphite, fiberglass and epoxy. The plausible theory is that less cumulative energy will be wasted over the course of 10,000 strokes during a three hour paddle. The trade off, of course, is that you won't be able use these hummingbird wings to push your canoe upriver or away from the beach, kill rattlesnakes, or use them as a filleting board.

Paddle Length

What about paddle length? One outdoor writer has quipped that, just as Abe Lincoln suggested a man's legs needed to be long enough to reach the ground, so a canoe paddle should be long enough to reach the water. The canoe tripper who will be taking long leisurely strokes, standing up in the canoe to survey the rapids and using the paddle as a pole from time to time, should choose a paddle which, when stood alongside on the floor, reaches to eye level or higher. The white-water and slalom enthusiast, on the other hand, will favor a paddle that is almost a foot shorter than chin-high. Until experience or a specialized requirement dictates otherwise, a stern paddle of chin height and a bow paddle six inches shorter will be comfortable for cruising of all sorts. For white water, you may wish to take a couple of inches off that.

LIFE PRESERVERS (PFDs)

Since 1971, the wearing of a Coast Guard–approved Personal Flotation Device (PFD) has been a matter of law, and with more and more people taking to the water, it's a good one. Brightly colored for good visibility, the PFD should be thought of as an article of clothing, like a ski parka or tennis shorts. In hot weather it can be worn with a bathing suit; in the cold, it acts like a down vest under a windbreaker or rain parka. And although its integrity as a life preserver may suffer ultimately, it makes a great cushion for sitting or even lying down at the lunch stop.

Look for a United States Coast Guard–approved Type III life jacket of either tube or panel construction. Avoid the "horse collars," which tend to chafe the neck and lack, in the case of cheap, non-USCG-approved models, sufficient flotation or adequate protection against rocks. The panel-type life jackets, usually filled with PVC foam (Ensolite), are somewhat more comforta-

Canoers should don life preservers (PFDs) as a matter of habit.

ble, but a number of models have a tendency to ride up in the water, in some cases dangerously so.

My own preference is for the tube type, filled with blocks of polyethylene foam and with a tie around the waist.

Getting the right size is important. Not only do you need sufficient flotation for your weight—and this should be indicated on the label—you should try the vest on for overall comfort.

Type III PFDs are a compromise between comfort and safety, since most will not keep an unconscious person fully face up in the water. The Coast Guard apparently reasoned that, in order to encourage canoers to use them, they would permit designs that would be worn cheerfully and comfortably. Your PFD should keep you in a semi-vertical position in the water, provide protection from the rocks, and not be a hindrance when swimming.

I have paddled a few miles in my life without a life jacket, and undoubtedly so will you. The Coast Guard can hardly be lurking behind every bush along every waterway, nor does every situation demand a PFD. Good judgment will suggest, however, that younger children, white-water boaters, and nonswimmers should always be protected. Keep in mind that a PFD can compensate only for your lack of buoyancy—not for your lack of common sense.

APPURTENANCES

With canoe, paddles, and life preservers you're ready to go—that's the beauty of canoeing.

A few other items are useful but not obligatory; as always, utility should be your primary consideration.

Lines

Whether tying up to a dock or a tree for a picnic or hauling the canoe up a riverbank, some good sturdy line is a necessity. Bow and stern lines are called painters. A few yards are probably adequate for most short jaunts; a canoe tripper might be wise to carry up to fifty feet.

Sponge and Bailer

A sponge is a good companion, even for paddling on a millpond when the sun is shining and your boat is completely leak-proof. Somehow, a little water

An old bleach bottle makes a great bailer. Note extra flotation for white-water paddling in this canoe.

always manages to collect in the bottom of your boat, whether off the paddle tip or brought in when you launch, and having a sponge quickly takes care of this annoyance. If you are going to be out in the elements, and certainly if there are going to be some rapids, both a sponge and a bailer are in order, conveniently tied to a thwart. Any large household sponge will do, although I have seen specially designed foam sponges, covered with terry cloth and with a small loop sewn on one corner so that it can be tied to a small line—a nifty idea. An old bleach bottle cut to form a scoop can bail a couple of inches of water out of a boat in no time, is practically weightless, and costs nothing.

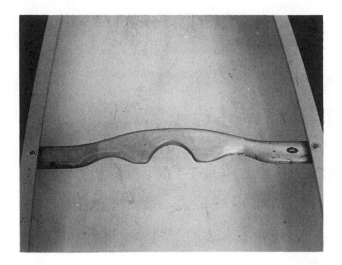

Carrying yokes can either be the commercial variety (above), permanently fitted midships in your canoe, or makeshift (right), using paddles tied in place. Life preservers or other padding can be used for carrying comfort.

Carrying Yoke

For carrying the canoe alone you will want a carrying yoke. You may either install a commercial variety or improvise with some nylon or cotton sash cord, using your canoe paddles and stuffing life preserver, sweater, or poncho between the cord and paddle blades to cushion the shoulders. For twenty years my canoes have had their little cords in place. This system has the added dividend of getting the paddles to wherever you are going without having to carry them separately.

Knee Pads

If you are going to be doing any white-water or extended canoeing, permanent or semi-permanent knee pads should be installed. Any closed-cell foam or neoprene can be used, cut into 10-inch squares and cemented into position with epoxy or contact cement. Temporary pads can be merely taped in place with duct tape. Paddlers of aluminum canoes, where adhesion is a problem, often wear painter's knee pads, which can be bought in any hardware store. For fussier folks, there are commercially available knee pads, or you may wish to carve form-fitting cups out of ethafoam blocks and cement them into your canoe.

Duct Tape

Canoers and white-water boaters, in particular, have come to depend on duct tape to such an extent that it is, as often as not, referred to as "boat tape." Since the tape has many other uses besides patching or protecting, it is probably all you'll need for most excursions, although my own kit also contains wire and a few nuts and bolts. In addition to patching small and large cracks, duct tape can be used to protect a paddle shaft from constant abrasion with the gunwale —and applied to the gunwale as well. It will patch a torn rain suit, broken-down tennis shoe, or broken beer cooler. I once saw two halves of a broken kayak rejoined on the river, and the boat finished the trip!

Waterproof Packs

Since you are going to be around water, and since you are likely to be carrying something with you, even if it is only your lunch, sooner or later you will need a waterproof bag or pack. The ultimate in canoe design may be reached, but

From gunwale-width "dry box" to pocket-size cases, hard-shelled packs will give you a good measure of security, especially when carrying fragile gear and crushables.

Tough waterproof bags come in many sizes, some with shoulder straps for heavy-duty portaging. Smaller bags might be consolidated in a large soft pack for portaging.

the search for perfection in watertight containers is never ending. Clear vinyl envelopes with Velcro enclosures, metal ammunition carriers, war-surplus hard rubber and canvas containers, double air-chambered transparent camera bags, rigid high-impact polystyrene boxes, four-peck rubberized white-water duffel bags, molded fiberglass gunwale-width boxes that take up a quarter of the canoe —these are just a few of the possibilities. After twenty years, I have at least one of each.

For carrying sensitive gear such as cameras, you will want either a rigid or hard pack or box, or one that inflates, so as to be able to withstand impact. The perfect combination of accessibility, durability, and absolute watertight integrity is yet to be discovered, but it's fun to watch the inventor's ingenuity at work. There are a number of hard-shelled boxes ranging from the gunwale-to-gunwale "Dry Box," down to the six-by-eight inch Pelican—and every size in between. A good bet for the camera gear is a fiberglass box with a gasketed lid, positive snapdowns, and foam lining that can be carved to hold camera body, lenses and other doodads.

Fragile items or not, the important considerations will be size or capacity, weight, durability, and reliability and ease of closure. Closures involving plastic sliders or roll-down-and-snap devices seem to seal more effectively than the pleats and tie or zipper arrangements. For the hard packs that use a rubber gasket, check the gasket periodically, since rubber will harden and crack in time.

At any rate, you should have fun seeking your "perfect" waterproof bag. You will no doubt be as successful as the skier who searches for "fog free" goggles.

The two-person carry—on the shoulders.

Getting Started

There are a few things you need to know even before you get your boat wet. Unless a canoe is kept tied up at a dock you are going to have to transport it to and from the water. We'll look at some boat-moving options and then learn some basic techniques.

TRANSPORTING THE CANOE

The canoe is nothing if not portable. Atop a sedan or station wagon, even a foam pad or an old blanket can serve as your "rack" for short distances; just make sure that your padding is under any part of the gunwales that might come in contact with the car.

To tie the canoe in place, use two lines over the top and far enough apart to distribute the tie-down pressure, yet not so far toward bow and stern as to lose their grip. Unless you use a rack, you will have to take the lines completely through the door or window openings.

A rope pulled straight down from both bow and stern to the bumper is OK if the canoe is firmly secured across the hull and if its lateral movement has been restricted. Better yet, form

Even smaller cars can easily accommodate a full-sized canoe. A line from bow to bumper will be next.

You need sturdy racks and taut lines, but with a rig like this, you'll save on shuttle cars.

equilateral triangles with a line drawn through the canoe bow to either end of the bumper and the same arrangement at the stern.

A good set of racks is your best bet. It is important to anchor them securely to the car. I speak from experience, having watched two of my prized wood and canvas canoes fly off the top of our car in a vicious side wind. The canoes were properly secured to the racks, but the racks weren't tied fast to the car. Everything flew off the rooftop, teaching me a hard lesson.

You can make your own racks from rain gutter clamps and two-by-four cross pieces, but a good canoe really deserves better: both Thule and Yakima make excellent racks, including a full complement of accessories, and both companies have models that attach to virtually every car or van roof, with or without rain gutters.

For tying down, use a good sturdy rope—not clothesline—of tightly woven cotton, hemp, or nylon, which permits you to get a good grip and which will hold a knot. Loose lines tend to get looser; there is no substitute for lines as taut and secure as you can make them. Make sure you periodically check these ropes for wear and either replace them or move the knots and friction points from time to time. Perhaps your bow and stern painters can double as tiedowns.

Two, three, or more canoes can be piled atop a car, but with each additional boat you add geometrically to the forces of wind, friction, weight, torque, and vibration brought to bear on your ropes and racks. No matter how many canoes you plan to carry, your objective should always be the same: to minimize slack and movement, be it the rack in relation to the car or the movement of the boats forward, sideways, and up and down.

The Shuttle

Unless you put into a lake, or a river with negligible current and paddle in a circle back to your point of departure, you are going to need a shuttle, a means of transportation waiting at the end, at your takeout point. For a downriver run or canoe trip of several days, arranging the shuttle may be as challenging as the trip itself. Obviously, you will need either one or more extra cars or a nonpaddling driver.

Because of shuttling, the self-propelled sport of canoeing all too often requires more than its share of gasoline. I have also tried motorbikes, ten-speed bicycles, shank's mare, and my thumb. For long trips, we have hired shuttle drivers to move our cars to a takeout distant from our launch point. More ambitious trips have required trains and float planes. These are all good reasons for joining a canoe club, where you are likely to find people going where you want to go or willing to follow you. Most clubs publish a trip schedule, detailing

For short distances, the two-person carry is fine. For a very short distance, such as dock to water, the carry opposite, using the knees, is OK.

dates, trips, leaders, and degree of difficulty. Through the leader, car pools can be coordinated and shuttle arrangements made.

CARRYING THE CANOE

For a short distance, it is an easy matter for two people to pick up a 70-pound canoe from each end and move it between car and water or even around a short portage such as at a dam. Use the bow and stern decks as handles or put the end of the boat into the crook of an arm or on the shoulder. The canoe can also be carried for short distances with one person on each side, as long as each person is the same distance from opposing ends of the canoe. (If your partner grabs the canoe by a thwart positioned four feet behind the bow, you will have to grab the gunwale or thwart on your side that is four feet ahead of the stern.)

One person can move a canoe a very short distance by using the knees as both lever and incline. This is especially appropriate for moving a canoe from land, or dock, to water. It is also the first and last positions in the one-person overhead carry.

One-Person Overhead Carry

The one-man portage is as much a part of canoe tripping as poling is to skiing. So it pays to figure it out and master it, even if your only canoe trips are to a neighborhood pond.

To get the canoe up on your shoulders, start by standing directly behind the midpoint of the canoe, its bottom resting on your knees. Next, put your left hand on the gunwale near you, just ahead of the center thwart, while reaching well down the center thwart with your right hand. Go slowly into a sitting position, knees well bent and your upper body counterbalancing the weight of the canoe, as you pry the canoe bottom up with your knees. At the same time, you will be pushing down on the gunwale with your left hand and pulling the thwart with your right, as you rotate the canoe on your thighs until its open hull is almost facing you and you are able to reach up and grab the opposite gunwale with your left hand. At this point you are holding the upper gunwale with your left hand about six inches ahead of the center thwart. Your right hand moves down to grip the thwart next to the lower gunwale.

Now comes the moment of truth, the clean and jerk. You will sink and recoil upward, pushing up your right hand (the lower gunwale), at the same time pulling down and steadying with your left hand on the left gunwale, and duck your head under that center thwart so it all comes to rest on the back of

A   B   C

One-Person Lift
Stand at the middle thwart and roll the canoe bottom up to rest against your
thighs (A). Reach down and grab the thwart (B) and then roll the canoe around
on your thighs (C). With the canoe facing you (D), and the canoe balanced on

your neck. If you are going to carry the canoe more than a short distance, it
makes sense to have a carrying yoke, either the commercially carved style or
the paddles and padding mentioned earlier.

Two-Person Overhead Carry

Some canoes have no center thwart—for reasons which elude me—in which
case you will either have to install one or resort to a two-person carry. The
two-person overhead carry is identical in execution to the one-person carry just
described, with the participants at either end of the canoe, but this is one
instance where theory and practice collide. While two would seem better than
one, by virtue of sharing the weight and eliminating the balancing act, the fact
is that for any distance beyond a few yards, one person can comfortably carry
a canoe a lot farther than two. More importantly, you won't be making a
lifelong enemy out of your seemingly misstepping partner, who invariably goes
up when you go down, zigs when you zag, or runs out of steam just as you catch
your second wind.

The best compromise and most effective utilization of two persons is to
have your partner hold up one end of an overturned canoe while you step under
the center thwart. Your partner lowers the canoe onto your shoulders, steadies
it, and you take off. At the end of the carry the sequence is reversed.

D   E   F

your thighs, reposition your hands, the upper on the gunwale and the lower on the thwart. Push up with your lower hand and pull down with your upper as you spring up from your crouching position and duck under the canoe (E), letting it come down to rest on your shoulders (F).

GETTING WATERBORNE

If your ideas of getting waterborne are modest ones, and if you are planning to learn canoeing one stroke at a time, read on. However, if you are already thirsting for the whitecaps of Great Bear Lake or the rapids of the Chattooga River, you would be advised to read chapter 8, "Safety and Fitness."

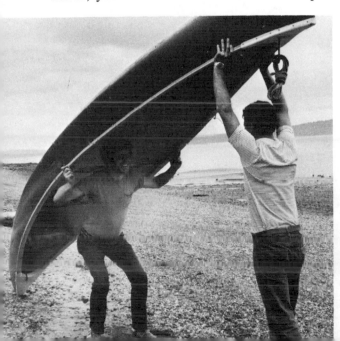

Your partner can hold up one end of the canoe while you get under and he can do the same when you go to put it down.

Paddling a canoe may be the most natural thing in the world, but getting into and out of a canoe seems to separate the initiated from the tyros. If you have a partner, one should hold the canoe for the other, preferably with the canoe fully afloat. While your partner steadies the canoe, you grasp the gunwales on either side and in front of your seat, step into the canoe, and lower yourself into the boat with most of the weight on your arms, not your feet. If circumstances, including the absence of a partner, require that you enter the canoe somewhere in the center, grasp the gunwales and move yourself forward or backward to your seat, advancing your hands along the gunwales as you go.

This does not mean that the canoe is such a precarious craft as to invariably require a precisely executed embarkation. You will often see able canoeists take all but flying leaps to and from their boats, creating hardly a ripple. But a proper technique should be mastered so that in those situations requiring finesse—such as loading on a windward shore as the incoming surf threatens to dash your canoe against the rocks—you will instinctively use the most conservative moves.

It is generally regarded as gauche to get into a canoe while it is on shore, and for some of the daintier models, including wood, this can put a severe crunch in the hull or backbone. Likewise, a canoe should be loaded while it is fully afloat; never load it on land and then drag it over rocks and gravel to the water.

To enter, grab the gunwales and move to your position as your partner steadies the canoe.

Getting Out of the Canoe

Another popular life-shortener is to run the canoe up on a beach. Adding insult to injury, some bow paddlers will hop out of the canoe and pull canoe, stern paddler, and all well up on shore; upon which the person in the stern must stand up in the teetering boat and move perilously up the canoe's back, suspended between water and shore. It's better to hold the boat, still fully in the water, as your partner disembarks.

Another common cartoon situation is the exit at shore or dockside in which one or both partners stand up in the boat and reach for the shore as they push the canoe out from under themselves. A variation has the paddler standing up and stepping out onto a shore that is suddenly not there, as the force of forward motion sends the canoe scooting away from shore and the unfortunate tyro into the water, two feet from the riverbank. Even for experienced canoers, getting into or out of the canoe is when you run the greatest risk of getting wet. Whatever the circumstance, there is no substitute for a thoughtful partner to hold the boat for both entries and exits.

To exit a canoe correctly, nudge it up to the bank, have your partner get out and steady the craft as you move forward, keeping low and holding on to the gunwales. (Below) How not to get out of a canoe. Note the precarious bridge between water and bank. This exit risks getting you wet and damaging the canoe as well.

If you have no partner, getting out of the boat calls for getting a good hold on the dock or shore and pulling yourself out, or using your paddle as an outrigger or crutch. A paddle laid across the gunwales, with its blade resting on the bank, can be used to support your full weight as you move from canoe to shore.

Trim

Now that you know how to get in and out of the canoe, let's discuss two other important subjects—trim and the positioning of people and gear to achieve optimum balance.

Trim refers to the position of the boat in relation to the water. A well-trimmed canoe is absolutely level from bow to stern and from gunwale to gunwale. There are circumstances when a *slightly* bow-heavy canoe is desirable, such as in a side wind, but such adjustments can wait until you have a better feel for canoeing. You will tend to have an efficient craft, under most conditions, if bow and stern are level. The most common problem usually involves an

A trim canoe is most efficient (A). Too much weight in the stern (B) may subject the canoe to windvaning.

A

B

unloaded canoe with a robust stern paddler and a petite bow partner. The canoe will pivot precariously on the rear quarter of the canoe bottom, like a kid doing a wheelie with a motocross bike—an attitude which is unstable and awkward and which can make even the attainment of stable forward motion difficult. Should this unmatched pair find themselves in a good breeze, they have a real problem.

If there is gear or duffel to be loaded, the solution to the problem is easy; equilibrium is achieved by adjusting the load toward the bow paddler. Another solution is to move the stern or bow seat forward.

Even the most unpracticed eye is going to recognize an unlevel canoe, and the solutions for attaining trim are usually obvious. What may be less obvious is the *importance* of a level canoe. If one is going to advance beyond pond paddling, it's as important as tight ski bindings or air in your bike tires.

For a single canoer, trim is best achieved by kneeling in front of the center thwart, with the buttocks resting on it. You should be positioned toward the side on which you will be paddling. Obviously, you will not be trim gunwale to gunwale, but that's the way it works. If you are going to sit, get on the bow seat and face the stern of the boat. By the way, if you are soloing in any but the calmest waters, you will have to get your bow down, either by placing a pack well forward or by kneeling in a position that accomplishes the same objective. It is even tougher for a single paddler to tame a "windvaning" canoe (so-called for the tendency of the canoe, like a wind vane, to pivot on its axis and point directly away from the wind). I've seen novice canoers go in one frustrating circle after another, for just a modest breeze can catch a bow and in a twinkling turn the whole boat away from the wind.

Center of Gravity

I defy you to tip a canoe over while lying in its bottom. This tells you all you need to know about the importance of a low center of gravity. Not surprisingly, a canoe with duffel on the floor is more stable than an empty canoe. Likewise, kneeling is a more secure position than sitting, and seats that are suspended three inches below the inwales (inside the gunwales) are going to give more stability than ones bolted just below the inwales. A long sleek racing boat tends to have its seats positioned lower, and one designed for tripping will tend to have them higher. The trip boat is likely to have gear as ballast, and its occupants are likely to put a premium on comfort if they will be sitting in a canoe for six hours; hence the higher seats.

The approach, then, is to load people and gear in such a manner as to achieve a trim canoe, with the weight concentrated as low as possible consistent with comfort. If you're going to have passengers, you will want them on the floor, not sitting up on the thwart, but some way should be devised to keep them off the bottom of the canoe. A boat seat or duffel will do the trick. If your passenger is a child, it is imperative to keep his or her behind off the cold bottom of the canoe and out of the inevitable collecting puddle.

Under way, on lake or river, and depending on the inherent stability of the canoe design, I adjust my position to reflect the degree of difficulty of the situation. Most of the time I'm sitting comfortably. But when winds and whitecaps begin to rise, or rapids are approached, my partner and I shift to our knees, buttocks resting against the seat. Not only have we lowered our center of gravity, we have increased our points of contact with the canoe, enabling us to use weight shifts as we both "ride" and control the pitch and direction of the craft.

In very heavy or violent rapids, or should we take in an inordinate amount of water, we will come away from our seats entirely, so that we are kneeling flat on the bottom of the canoe, buttocks on our heels. If you should ship water, particularly in the absence of gear or other ballast, you will find just two inches sloshing from side to side makes a boat intolerably unstable. As uncomfortable as it may be, that's the time to get well down on your knees and get to shore, where you can bail or empty the canoe as soon as possible.

Never stand up in a canoe except when it's necessary and appropriate to

To cope with heavy water, the stern paddler has dropped low on his knees.

Rapids ahead. Standing up in a canoe has its uses.

do so, such as scouting the rapids ahead. Experienced canoers stand up in their canoes all the time, just as bikers ride with their hands off the handlebars, but presumably they have reached the point of proficiency and harmony with their vehicle where virtuosity or the requirements of the situation make it appropriate. Since standing in a canoe violates the low-center-of-gravity principle, you ultimately will have to be the judge as to when such a maneuver is called for. Like every other rule in this book, you should read, follow the instructions, and, when mastery is achieved, make up your own rules. If you accomplish your purpose and do not pitch headlong into the lake, then standing meets the rules of "appropriateness."

It is easier to make a canoe go in a straight line if it is well trimmed and properly loaded. We will cover a multitude of techniques in the next chapters, but you need to know a few other things right now so that you can get the boat on the water. Remember that strokes are presented in sequence. Each level must be mastered before a new technique can be learned.

A   B   C

THE POWER STROKE

To get going, you need a straight power stroke. Grasp the top of your canoe paddle palm down, putting your lower hand down the paddle shaft as close to the blade as possible without having your hand in the water. Both bow and stern paddlers should lean forward at the waist and extend their arms. Lead with the lower hand, followed by a forward punch with the upper hand, to put the paddle blade into the water ahead of you on the same side as your lower hand; then pull the boat forward, describing a reasonably straight line with the canoe paddle parallel to the keel line. Bring your upper body back with the paddle blade. If you are in the bow, pull the paddle out as it reaches your hips. In the stern, carry your blade farther back, depending on your need to execute one of the correcting strokes (described later). As the paddle blade comes out of the water, twist the shaft to "feather" the blade (turn the blade surface horizontal to the water to reduce air resistance) for its return and the start of the next stroke.

Sternman

Bowman

D

The Power Stroke
This stroke uses both back and arms (A). Paddler punches out with the upper hand (B), pulls the paddle out of the water just past the hips (C), and feathers it (D) for return to the next stroke.

Which Side?

For the traditionalist, the so-called Northwoods paddler and the whitewater paddler, partners generally pick a side and stick with it. Performance minded, fast cruisers and racing paddlers (see Chapter 7 for a full discussion) may prefer to "hit 'n switch." For the moment, think about choosing one side or the other. Your paddling side is like your throwing arm, but it does not necessarily follow that a right-handed thrower will feel more comfortable paddling on the right. For me, it just happens to be the opposite. Happiness is finding a canoeing partner whose natural side is the opposite of yours. There are plenty of paddlers, however, who have had to become proficient on their other side: usually compliant spouses or intimidated guest paddlers.

The stern paddler should not resort to changing sides in order to make the canoe go straight—or to go in any direction, for that matter. This in spite of the fact that within three strokes your canoe will start veering off to the right if you, in the stern, are paddling on the left, your partner on the right. Why? Because most canoes (unless they are designed to go in a straight line, such as a racing boat) are somewhat directionally unstable, but, more importantly, because your position in the extreme stern of the canoe gives you much greater leverage than the bow

A   B

position. Think of the ease with which a tire lug is loosened with a good long-handled tire iron, and you will understand the principle: The paddler in the stern is well out on the end of the lever.

THE STERN PRY

The easiest and most reliable response to correct and offset this strong tendency of the canoe to veer away from your paddling side is the stern pry, or rudder, also referred to as a pushaway stroke.

At the end of your power stroke, when your lower hand is well behind your seat, put the heel of that hand on the gunwale and turn your upper hand palm outward, in order to pull firmly on the grip of your newly created lever. Your lower hand holds your lever in place on the gunwale, which acts as a fulcrum as you pull the grip toward your chin and "pry" the stern of the boat toward you—thus straightening out the boat.

Only practice and adjustment to your particular boat and bow partner will tell you how often and with what degree of force to apply your lever, but generally you will need to make a compensating stern pry every two to three strokes. Needless to say, a continued or vigorous application of the stern pry will turn your boat sharply toward your paddling side, so that it is more than just a correcting stroke. Some paddlers put the paddle shaft right on the

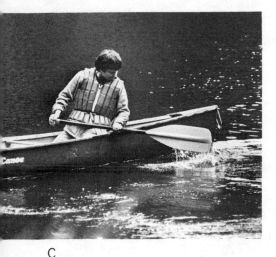

C

The Stern Pry
The stern paddler puts the paddle shaft against the gunwale (A) and (B) pulls the handle toward her, thus prying the stern over (C). The sequence can be repeated or power strokes commenced until a correcting pry is required.

gunwale (rather than using the heel of their hand as a buffer); while this method is a little tough on paddles and gunwales, positive leverage is dramatically increased.

The stern pry is not as classy as the J stroke, which is covered in the next chapter, but the potential force with which it can be applied makes it more dynamic and useful. By adjusting the pitch of the paddle blade—using your upper hand—and varying the vigor of your lever, you can achieve a full range of effects, from a gentle ruddering action to an abrupt directional change and slowing of the boat. Continuing to "push away" with the back of your paddle blade, following a stern pry, will continue to turn your canoe in the direction of your paddling side.

THE STERN SWEEP

From time to time, because of winds, the current, or your bow paddler's action, you will need to turn your bow more forcefully *away* from your paddling side. This is accomplished by "sweeping" the paddle blade in an arc, slightly fore and well aft of you; your paddle shaft is now extended out over the water, instead of perpendicular to the gunwale, and only a quarter to a half of the blade is in the water. Here again, exerting maximum force near the completion of the arc will sharpen the canoe's response.

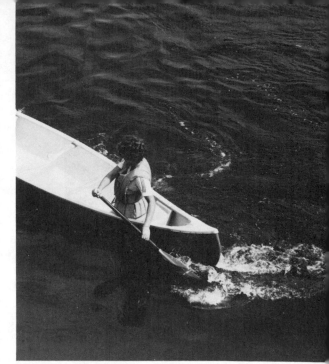

A
B

GROUP LESSONS

In recent years clinics for all grades of paddling have sprung up. These are offered by canoe clubs, dealers, community colleges, and outdoor recreation schools patterned after the Outward Bound programs, and while they may range from semi-volunteer operations—such as those offered by local canoe clubs—to slickly promoted productions, they are well worth looking into. Canoeing lends itself to group instruction, and, unlike skiing, no one gets left behind.

While a particular course may emphasize river canoeing, or canoe camping, the good ones will concentrate on teaching judgment in addition to equipment requirements, paddling techniques, and safety practices. The "follow me" or "sink-or-swim" mode of instruction is something to be avoided.

Since the fullest enjoyment of canoeing—as well as the safest—comes from the tandem partnership between family members or friends, learning in a group provides an instant assemblage of like-minded people. Students might range in age from 10 to 60; a good student-teacher ratio is 5 to 1. That means the instructor has one student in his or her boat and must watch only two other boats. A good rule is that no couples, roomies, brothers, sisters, or friends paddle together, and every effort should be made to switch students among

The Stern Sweep
The stern sweep starts well out
from the boat (A), and gets its
maximum power as the blade is
pulled toward the stern of the
canoe (B).

different boats, different partners, different paddle sides, and each end of the
canoe.

The early sessions on pond and pool will emphasize boat control, maneuvering—perhaps even races—among buoys, paddling backward, and paddling
sideways. Kneeling at poolside, students may practice sweeps, draws, pries,
and, finally, braces. The last are executed in the extreme to see how far they
can go before falling in. Tipping over a lot in the canoe is also part of the
learning and familiarization process. Dipping the gunwales to see how close
they can come to touching the water without actually going over heightens
awareness.

Later on the river—if that is the emphasis—an easy but varied stretch will
be chosen. Every current, every eddy, every obstacle will be worked and re-
worked. Perhaps the same one-mile stretch of water will be run several times.
Sides, ends, and paddlers will be switched. Getting dumped is part of the drill,
and chilly waters make fast learners out of the less gifted. Group dynamics and
healthy competition provide additional impetus to the learning process.

For those of us who survived the sink-or-swim school of canoeing, it is
gratifying to see these clinics growing in number and popularity. I would
strongly recommend aspiring paddlers to seek them out. There is absolutely no
substitute for getting wet under controlled and safety-oriented conditions.

4

Skills for Quiet Water

The canoeing strokes I was taught as a kid, and which were depicted in the popular manuals (many of which still survive in print), now appear stilted, a trifle unnatural, and passive. It would have never occurred to me that the paddle could also be used as a powerful lever, as a support for the weight of an entire canoe, or as an outrigger, permitting the negotiating of seas and cascades which in years past would have been avoided by all but the most brash.

Today we think about paddles and strokes in new ways for we know that water can be leaned on, pushed off of, and used to pull a canoe in any direction. Formerly canonized strokes such as the bow rudder and cross-bow rudder will not be found here. Our thesis is that fewer is better and that perfection of the newer strokes and their variations will provide the arsenal necessary for tackling any kind of water.

As you gain proficiency, get out over your paddle; don't be afraid to put your full weight on it. Next, observe the principles of leverage to maximize your control over the boat; apply your paddle-blade power as far from the canoe's pivot point as possible and maximize your grip on the canoe (by kneeling, for example). Use the natural lever

69

Today's strokes are active but natural.

A　　　　　　　　　　B　　　　　　　　　　C

The J Stroke
The J stroke starts underwater (A) and both upper and lower wrists are rolled forward (B) so that the power face of the blade "catches" and straightens out the canoe. C and D show blade coming out of the water feathered to return for next stroke. Closeup in E shows wrists rolled forward and power face of paddle pushing away.

of paddle shaft and gunwale. Finally, use your back and upper body, moving your torso forward and backward with your strokes or out over the water for your draws and sweeps.

Kneeling

While your time on quiet waters will be mostly in a sitting position, you would do well to learn the strokes from a kneeling position. With a lower center of gravity and knee contact with the hull, you are in a better position to make vigorous and positive moves, reaching well out from the canoe on your draws and sweeps without worrying about balance. If you think about paddle strokes as a means of moving the canoe rather than moving water, the leverage advantage resulting from increased contact with the boat becomes apparent. It's the difference between grabbing the jack handle in your fist or using your thumb and index finger. After you've mastered the strokes and absorbed the principles involved, you can get up on the seat and relax.

Note: Strokes are described for two canoeing partners, with observations, where appropriate, about solo paddlers in the same situation.

D   E

THE J STROKE

Up to this point, the bow paddler has been performing a basic forward stroke, oblivious to your struggle, with pries and sweeps, to stay on a straight course. We will commit your partner to this oblivion a bit longer while we push you even farther out into the lake, using a J stroke.

The J stroke is harder to perfect and lacks the power potential of the stern pry, but for quiet paddling and long distances, where a change of pace or a resting stroke is desirable, it is both valuable and pleasing. Unlike the stern pry, which can be executed exclusive of a forward stroke, the paddler sows the seed of the J almost immediately after a forward stroke is under way.

While the stern pry, or pushaway, uses the nonpower face of the paddle blade (that is, the blade facing away from you on your power or straight forward stroke), the J utilizes the power face, which, shortly after you start your forward stroke, is pitched outward through a combination of wrist and paddle actions. Halfway between the start of your stroke and where you reach your hips, roll your lower wrist sharply inward (forward) and drive the paddle deeper into the water as your upper and lower grips coordinate to turn the inside edge of the blade sternward, so that you can pull the power face of the blade up and away from the canoe with your lower arm. The simultaneous

Stern Sweep and Bow Draw
The stern sweep as the bow draws will cause this canoe to circle sharply to the left.

downward push and twist of the paddle shaft is the key; you will feel the blade "catch" as it makes its "J." There is a natural transition from the final upward part of the J as the blade is withdrawn from the water, already in a feathered position and poised for the next stroke.

Only with practice and many miles of paddling will this stroke become natural to you, as you unconsciously adjust the motions and the amount of power applied to accomplish a smooth forward thrust.

STERN SWEEP AND BOW DRAW

It's time to bring the bow into the act. Your most effective stroke is the stern pry; for the bow paddler, it is the draw. The two are antagonistic, as opposed to complementary, so if the bow is to initiate the turn homeward, you can provide a complementary sweep as the bow paddler draws the paddle blade toward the boat, causing the boat to turn *away* from your paddling side.

To execute the draw, the paddler reaches as far out as caution permits, jabbing the paddle blade into the water on the same plane as the keel line and pulling the paddle toward the canoe, making sure to pull it out of the water well before it reaches the canoe. Several jabs and draws by the bow paddler—really, "drawing" the canoe to the paddle—coupled with a stern sweep will pivot the boat smartly. The stern paddler could also substitute a stern draw for the sweep, recognizing that it is the final part of the stern sweep that provides the real turning impetus. The stern draw is the same as the bow draw, but is executed somewhat behind the stern paddler's hips. With experience, you will refine your techniques and develop your own preferences.

The beginner's tendency in the draw is merely to extend the arms and twist the paddle blade, but the grip and orientation of the paddle to your grip need not change. You must turn your whole upper body from the hips and extend both your head and arms out over the water, your eyes on the paddle shaft, to plant the paddle as far out from the boat as possible.

STERN PRY AND BOW SWEEP

At the stern paddler's whim, or if a turn in the other direction is called for by route or circumstance, the turn may be initiated with the *stern* power stroke —the stern pry. The complementary bow stroke is the bow sweep.

Stern Pry and Bow Sweep
The stern pry and the bow sweep causes
the canoe to turn sharply to the left. Note
bow paddler leaning well forward to get
maximum leverage on his sweep.

The bow sweep is much the same stroke as the stern sweep described in
chapter 3, but now the bow paddler gains leverage by reaching the paddle tip
as far out in front of the boat as possible and "sweeping" the paddle in a broad
arc. As with the stern sweep, however, the arc can be shortened so that the
principal power is applied as far out on the lever as possible; that is, well in front
of the boat.

This stroke—in fact, all the basic strokes—can be used repeatedly to
achieve the most punch at the point of maximum leverage in the stroke. Thus
the stern may give three or four sharp pries in succession, as the bow paddler
jabs the sweep out in front of the canoe, reaching with back and arms to pull
the bow around. On the other hand, if your pace is leisurely, you can initiate
your turn, and most general-purpose canoe designs, being directionally unstable, will tend to continue it. (A V-hull deep-keeled canoe, however, is going to
require a more persistent technique.)

Earlier, we had the stern paddler substitute a draw for a sweep. Likewise, in this complementary pair, the stern may do a reverse sweep as an alternative to the pry. For the reverse sweep the stern paddler uses the nonpower face of the paddle to carve an upside-down arc in the water as the paddle pushes the water away from the stern of the canoe.

An option: the reverse sweep and bow sweep.

You now have all the strokes you will ever need for quiet waters, and there are legions of canoers who get by on less—such as letting the stern paddler make all the moves! But to advance beyond unruffled waters, you and your partner need to perfect the sweep, the stern pry, and the bow draw and bow sweep, and ideally you will each take the time to learn the other's strokes.

REVERSE

To this point we have gone only in a forward direction, but your canoe has a "reverse" as well. On quiet water, strokes to reverse direction are seldom needed except for moving away from shore, maneuvering in or out of a tight corner, or docking. Often, "full astern" is accomplished by a good shove with the paddle tip off the bank or beach. While on quiet water, you and your partner should practice going in reverse, just by using the nonpower face of your canoe paddle. Your paddle positions for back paddling (something you may use later for getting around river bends) will be the same as in the forward power stroke, but you will be like a movie in reverse. Your strokes will also be shorter.

It will be a simple matter for both of you to propel the boat backward for a few yards, but it takes real teamwork to accomplish a straight line or turns in both directions. For serious white-water paddlers and slalom racers, mastery is essential. I could fill the next few pages with diagrams, but they would be more confusing than constructive. It's something you should experiment with, especially if you think you're headed for the world of white water.

The solo paddler, sitting on the bow seat, facing the stern, or kneeling in front of the center thwart, can manage all the necessary turns and maneuvers described for tandem paddlers with J stroke, stern pry, and stern sweep, observing earlier admonitions about windvaning, should a breeze come up.

5

Skills for Moving Water

The same canoe that can be totally forgiving on a small lake under gentle breezes can become a stubborn or frisky critter when waters begin to move. A familiar story is the novice canoer who heads off down the lake with a nice tail wind and, if able to turn around at all, finds that the two miles covered in forty-five minutes by coasting downwind now entail two hours of head-down digging, which neither the novice's muscles nor skills are up to. If breezes are stiff or gusting, paddlers just trying to come about are going to have a struggle on their hands, particularly if they are light in the bow.

Wind is the canoeist's most frustrating adversary. There is only one technique for dealing with heavy winds and white-capped waters: Avoid them! Until you know the limits of your ability, err on the side of conservatism. A canoe weighing 70 pounds and presenting a broad surface is highly vulnerable to the wind. At best, strong breezes will hamper your forward progress; at worst, they can raise seas sufficient to swamp your boat or commit you to a course not of your choosing.

Avoidance does not mean total abstinence; a strategy designed to minimize the effects of wind should be your objective. If you must paddle, stay as close to land as is practical and try to use a lee shore (out of the wind), if available. One learns from experience, however, that on larger bodies of water the wind and its effects tend to conform to the configuration of the lake, so that a west wind can seem to come from three directions at once, making progress difficult for a canoe headed southwest, west, or northwest. In a channel or river that trends to the northwest, a west wind will funnel through the valley created by the channel, so that you in your canoe will perceive it as a northwest wind.

Nonetheless, your strategy will be one of seeking the lee shores and hugging them to minimize the consequences of a swamping. All this may sound ominous, so I hasten to say that in thirty years of canoeing we have never been swamped, nor have any of my acquaintances. But the danger exists, and your awareness and good judgment are the best safeguards.

The greatest danger is the sudden rising of a squall or thunderstorm with canoers committed to the open reaches of a large lake and far from shore. A nose for changing weather is a good ally.

QUARTERING

The strokes for coping with windy waters are essentially no different from those already described, but positiveness of execution and mastery of paddling a straight line gives you an edge. Obviously, a zigzagging canoe is an inefficient one, requiring extra energy you can ill afford in such circumstances and providing more opportunities for the wind to snatch or shove at your bow.

A kneeling position should be your first tactic. Next comes the orientation of your canoe to the waves, analogous to "tacking" in a sailboat. You need to pick the best line: basically, the route that achieves your objective (a dock, point of land, or lee shore) without putting your broadside to the waves or committing you even further to windy reaches of the lake.

The tactic here is known as "quartering," and whether you are running with or paddling against the wind, your canoe's steerage and stability are improved by moving obliquely to the line of the waves.

The quartering tactic lengthens the peaks and troughs of the waves and tends to lessen the precipitous rise and fall of bow and stern which results from hitting the waves straight on. It's usually the slap into the trough that puts a bucketful of water in the bow paddler's lap.

Running with the wind is also best done at a quartering angle. It is one of the great sensations in canoeing, but it also presents challenges. Depending on your canoe, its load, and your headway, you will get some "surfing" action, but as the following seas build, you will find yourself sliding off the backs of

Quartering into the waves is the best way to paddle against the wind.

the waves, your stern sinking into the trough, as the next breaking wave threatens to wash over the gunwales, right at the stern seat.

Your paddle strokes heading into the wind must be deliberate and, for the stern paddler, correcting strokes must be applied forcefully while paying attention to the angle of attack. Here is an instance where you may want to ignore earlier suggestions that you and your partner pick a paddling side and stick with it. Two paddlers quartering into the waves and paddling on their strong sides may well find that a switch to the opposite sides will mean more effective use of the stern pry, the stern's strongest stroke. And yet there are some combinations of wind velocity and direction, wave action, quartering angle, canoe trim, and relative strength of bow and stern paddler that make it easier to paddle just as is, the stern paddler discovering that a pry or rudder need be applied only occasionally, with a stern sweep added every now and then to keep the canoe from veering broadside into the trough.

Running both against and with the wind, there is some danger of spinning on the top of a wave, so the bow and stern paddlers may want to use their pry

A

B

Stern Pry and Bow Cross Draw
Together, the stern pry and bow cross drawn turn the canoe here sharply to the right (A,B). In C, the bow paddler from his normal paddling position, without changing his grip, swings his paddle across the bow and plants it well out from the opposite side of the canoe.

and draw, respectively, as bracing or outrigging. One or the other paddler must have firm purchase on some piece of water. In the stern, you can convert your stern pry into a brace by moving the heel of your hand (in the prying sequence) back, or off the gunwale, twisting the paddle blade with your lower hand to put the nonpower face flat on the water, and putting your weight on it. You have just created an outrigger.

The bow paddler likewise may use the draw stroke, not as a means of turning the canoe but of also creating an outrigger. In white water these techniques will be refined and carried further.

THE CROSS DRAW

We will cover white-water techniques in chapter 7, but there are many little streams, offering delightful canoeing, whose tight bends can be as challenging as a slalom course. A moderate current compounds the challenge. Anticipation

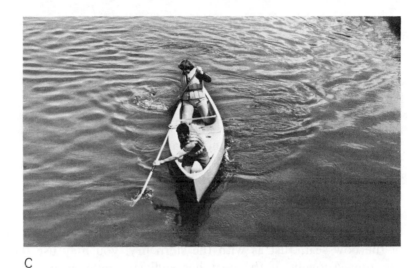

C

—making your moves before you are too far into the bend—will put you mostly in control. More than a few experienced canoers have ended up tangled in the alders on the outside of a tight little bend, so be prepared to take a few of those turns with good humor.

The stern pry is your staple, and for tight turns to your off side it's time to break the rules again: Switch paddling sides and pry away. In these situations the person in the bow really works and should, in fact, be the one to anticipate and initiate the appropriate moves, which includes watching out for the inevitable snags that are a part of little-river canoeing. The bow paddler's draw stroke must be sharper and more anticipatory, and a new stroke, the cross draw, must be mastered.

The bow paddler does not change grips for this stroke, but turns the entire upper body and shoulders toward the off-paddling (opposite) side, swinging the paddle up and over the bow, the elbow of the upper paddling arm tucked into the side. The bow paddler then extends the lower arm and trunk to plant the blade well out from the canoe. As with the draw, the end of the canoe is pulled to the paddle and the blade is quickly raised from the water before it goes under the boat.

So much for the little streams. They're fun, and every bend can bring a fresh surprise. Remember that the current is fastest at the outside of a bend, and that there are plenty of opportunities to get in a jam. So make sure you have your strokes down pat on flat water.

THE BOW PRY

Most of the important interchangeable strokes have been discussed, such as stern sweep and stern draw and stern pry and reverse sweep. Now let's look at an alternative to the cross draw, the bow pry. You may want to experiment with it, since some people find it a little tricky, particularly in fast-moving or heavy water, but it is effective!

There should be some forward momentum of the canoe; then you push the blade straight down into the water, on a plane with the keel line and well ahead of the bow seat. Just as with the stern pry, you may use the gunwale as a fulcrum. Actually, if the boat has sufficient momentum, and especially in fast-moving water, just holding the blade perpendicular while leaning *away* (downstream, if you're on a river) will move your bow over smartly.

PADDLING RIVERS WITH GRADIENT

Gradient is simply the total feet of altitude drop of a river, or the section to be run, divided by the number of miles under consideration. Thus a river that drops 100 feet in 100 miles has a one-foot-per-mile gradient, which translates into a very moderate current. Assuming the gradient is constant, a one-to-four-foot gradient per mile would, in all likelihood, have very little white water. You had better be certain that the gradient applies to the river section you are running, however. The Fond du Lac River in northern Saskatchewan has only a two-foot drop per mile over its 250-mile distance, but there are lake expansions of oceanlike proportions along its route, so that most of the drop takes place in narrower sections of the river, where roaring cataracts and incredible waterfalls render these sections unrunnable.

To develop new skills, consider low-gradient rivers but ones with a good solid current, perhaps 4 to 8 mph. The Yukon, for example, would run in the upper part of that range. Such rivers are also known as Class I, defined by the International Scale of River Difficulty as "moving water with a few riffles and small waves. Few or no obstructions." (See chapter 8 for the complete classification.)

THE BACK FERRY

Your principal concern on such rivers will be sand or gravel bars and "sweepers"—obstacles such as brush or fallen trees that allow the current through but can trap your canoe. As you have learned from the little rivers, the current is fastest toward the outside of a bend. Often this is where the sweepers lodge, reaching far out into the water and representing an obstacle—indeed, a danger —to the canoer. By positioning yourself well before you get into the turn, and letting the current work for you, you can negotiate the big bends easily. The specific technique is known as the "back ferry," or setting around a bend.

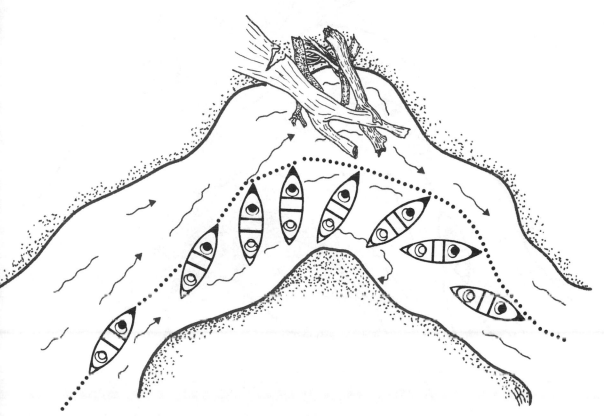

Back ferry: setting around a bend.

In the back ferry, the canoe doesn't make its turn until well into the bend, since you hold the canoe in a position relative to the direction of the current rather than to the shore. By putting your canoe into reverse, back paddling, you can keep to the inside of the bend until you are much of the way through; the naturally faster current coming from the outside of the bend gives the bow of the canoe a shove in the right direction. This is a maneuver that can only be learned on the water, and the speed of the current and configuration of the river will dictate your angle of attack and the force of your back paddle. It is also worth knowing what *not* to do: Don't paddle with a full head of steam into the bend and become overcommitted to the outside before it's too late. You want to have your boat moving slower than the current as you make the turn.

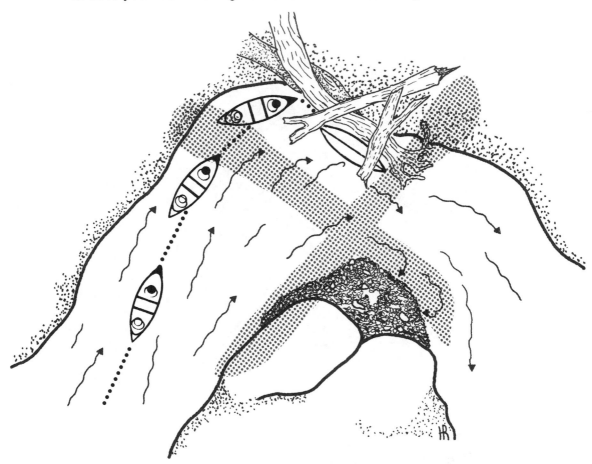

Danger of canoe becoming overcommitted to outside of bend.

Other Ways Around

If you and your partner are not yet a well-oiled machine capable of coordinating both the strength of the back paddle and the correct angle of the canoe—or if the inside of the bend is filled by a gravel bar—you may find the back ferry is impractical. Often the gravel bar forces you into a narrow channel and toward the outside of the bend. In this case, you may enter the top of the channel with your bow well angled toward the inside of the bend. At times, and depending on the speed of the river or the steepness of the gradient, you may be almost broadside to the current, attempting to ride the inside edge of the main current (specifically, the eddy line described in chapter 6) and straightening out the canoe as soon as the obstacle is passed.

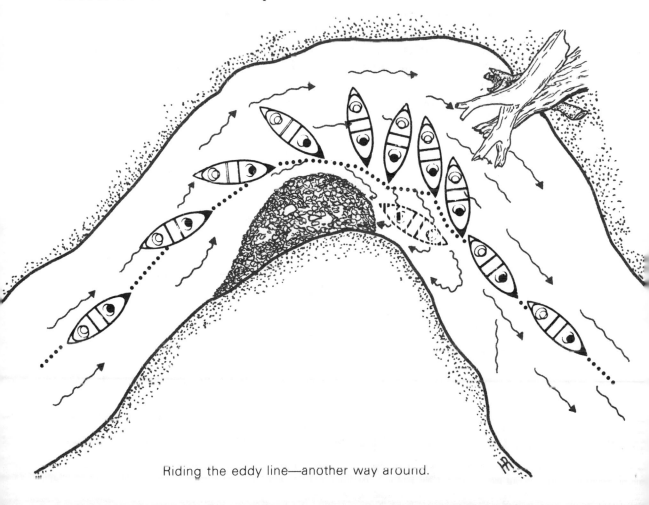

Riding the eddy line—another way around.

If the outside of the bend contains an unnerving entanglement of logs or debris, or if the currents are persuasively strong and you want to play it conservatively, there is still another ploy: Not only do you bring your canoe broadside as you move down the channel, you get your bow pointed upstream and cross over the eddy line into the backwater below the bar on the inside of the bend. If you should cross the eddy line before your bow is angled upstream, be prepared to lean to the inside of your turn. The technique, known as eddying in, is described in greater detail in chapter 6.

THE UPSTREAM FERRY

Another maneuver, and one which helps explain the principles involved in the back ferry (although not designed to get you around river bends), is the upstream ferry. This has two main purposes on a fast-moving river: one is to permit you to hit a shoreline target as you move downriver; the other is to get you from one side of the river to the other—that is, directly across—without being swept far downstream. The principle used is the same as that of the

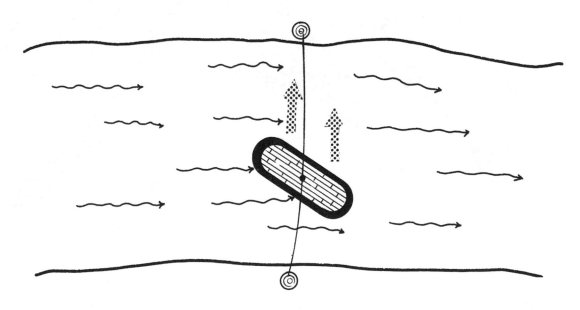

The ferryboat illustrates the principle of the upstream ferry.

oldtime ferry, which had only river current as its motive power. Tethered to
a stationary cable stretched across the river, the ferry moved directly across
under the cable by being angled right or left, according to the direction of the
onrushing river current.

Instead of the cable and tether, the paddlers of a canoe must provide
sufficient headway to maintain the angle which will allow the river current to
move the canoe straight across. It's the angle that's important; if you have to
paddle too hard, your angle is wrong. In general, the stronger the current, the
more acute the angle.

The upstream ferry is probably the most useful tactic in all river canoeing.
It should be practiced at every opportunity and mastered before any rivers of
consequence are attempted. While there is much Class I water that can be
enjoyed without this tool, it is a must for white water of all grades, and a
technique you will want to take on any canoe trip involving large rivers with
gradient.

An Introduction to Fast Water

Learning to read rivers is an important skill for any canoeist, whether you are planning to tackle white water or not. This chapter will discuss faster water in general and then describe skills necessary for running it.

WATER VOLUME

Class II water, according to the International Scale of River Difficulty, contains "easy rapids with waves up to three feet, and wide clear channels that are obvious without scouting. Some maneuvering is required." Class III water has "rapids with high irregular waves often capable of swamping an open canoe, and narrow passages that often require complex maneuvering. Many require scouting from shore." In general, Class III water is only suitable for open canoes at lower water levels. Class III should be considered the upper limit of navigability for canoes unless they have decking of some sort and additional flotation.

The classification of a river is a function of its gradient and of obstacles such as boulders, ledges, and narrow chutes. These indigenous features tell us the river's potential, but it is the volume of

Preparing for the next drop, two paddlers maneuver for position in Class II water.

water that creates the reality. One so-called Class II river, when swollen by rains or spring runoff, can become precarious for an open canoe; another Class II river with different features may well flatten out at high-water levels, as rocks and ledges are covered, and paddlers here can look forward to a big, fast, yet relatively safe ride.

Handling High Water

While different riverbed configurations will react differently to high volumes of water flow, it is best to start off by assuming that high water will increase a river's degree of difficulty. Never underestimate the power of moving water. Its force appears to increase geometrically as volume increases; thus, the strength and swiftness of stroke execution must likewise be increased. The consequences of a capsize in high water can be severe, as canoers struggle against a powerful current and their swamped canoe, weighing the equivalent of two tons of hydraulic force, lumbers downstream. Although obstacles are fewer in high water, the reaction time to avoid those remaining is greatly shortened, and the associated turbulence is substantially increased.

Handling Low Water

Low water levels, on the other hand, bring their own special problems. Boulders and ledges that were covered by higher water are now revealed in profusion; maneuvering becomes more complex. However, you will have more time to react, since your canoe is not moving as fast, and the consequences of a dump are not as severe. Currents, eddies, and standing waves—soon to be discussed —are more benign and forgiving of poor technique.

KNOW YOUR RIVER

Local reports provided by knowledgeable people are your best guide to classification. Knowledgeable people are those who recognize *your* skill level and who have run the river recently in a boat similar to yours. People who live on the river are likely to be unreliable too, unless they are canoers; they can be either too optimistic about a river's navigability or overly conservative. Ready to start down a sizable river in Quebec, our crew sought out an Indian who had lived along its banks all his life. His ominous description of the river and its perilous course would have caused any sane person to abandon the expedition forthwith. Once under way, however, we relied on our own scouting and judgment. The river was challenging, but hardly unrunnable.

INTERNATIONAL SCALE OF RIVER DIFFICULTY
(From AWA Safety Code)

If rapids on a river generally fit into one of the following classifications, but the water temperature is below 50°F, or if the trip is an extended one into wilderness area, the river should be considered one class more difficult than normal.

CLASS I Moving water with a few rifles and small waves. Few or no obstructions.

CLASS II Easy rapids with waves up to 3 feet and wide, clear, channels that are obvious without scouting. Some maneuvering is required.

CLASS III Rapids with high, irregular waves often capable of swamping an open canoe. Narrow passages that often require complex maneuvering. May require scouting from shore.

CLASS IV Long, difficult rapids with constricted passages that often require precise maneuvering in very turbulent waters. Scouting from shore is necessary, and conditions make rescue difficult. *Generally not possible for open canoes.* Boaters in covered canoes and kayaks should have the ability to Eskimo roll.

CLASS V Extremely difficult, long, and very violent rapids with highly congested routes, which always should be scouted from shore. Rescue conditions are difficult, and there is significant hazard to life in the event of a mishap. Ability to Eskimo roll is essential for boaters in kayaks and decked canoes.

CLASS VI Difficulties of Class V carried to the extreme of navigability. Nearly impossible and very dangerous. For teams of experts only, after close study has been made and all precautions have been taken.

UNSUITABLE FOR OPEN CANOES

Being able to read water is a prerequisite for running rapids.

River guidebooks, if they have been conscientiously written by someone who has run the river within the last five years, can be a helpful starting point. Next, check with a member of a local canoe club who has either run the river recently or has information from someone who has. Remember, though, that much misinformation is dispensed, and reports that are valid are often ignored by would-be canoeists. On crowded waters, if air and water temperatures are warm and potential rescuers numerous, the novices who are over their heads —actually and figuratively—can be fished out. With increasing frequency, unfortunately, the consequences can be tragic, as more and more canoers with no knowledge of either canoeing basics or safety precautions tackle strange rivers. Know the water you are running, and take with you the requisite skills.

READING WATER

Most Class II water can be run by competent paddlers without scouting—if your information is accurate! Most Class III water, on the other hand, probably requires scouting before running, unless you are following a competent leader who knows the river. Scouting a section of river determines the best route around or through a series of obstacles—or if the section should be run at all. A downed tree from a recent storm, an unrunnable ledge exposed by lower-than-normal water, or dangerously high standing waves created by high water may lead to a decision to carry around a particular stretch.

What exactly are you looking for? If one were to conduct a controlled laboratory experiment, whereby a flow of water was directed with even velocity down a perfectly straight line, etched in a solid but yielding bed such as clay, one would discover after some period of time that the "river" would begin to oscillate, or meander, rhythmically. Of course, real rivers do not descend absolutely uniform gradients through uniform mediums. In addition to clay of varying density, there are gravels, loose soil, formations of sandstone and shale, and obstacles created by intrusive geologic formations. All these features give the river its character, but it is the river's tendency to oscillate, all else being equal, that governs its existence.

As you spend more time on a river, you become increasingly aware of how its main current moves back and forth; first left, undercutting the bank; then seeming to bounce off in the opposite direction; then sweeping in a new arc into the right bank. As you come to recognize the rhythm of river currents, their anomalies, and their interruptions and irregularities, the apparent contradictions become more understandable.

Haystacks are standing waves created by the collision of fast water with the slower water at the bottom of a drop.

Haystacks

Generally speaking, the current will be faster at the center of the river in straight sections and slower near the banks. Yet as you approach a bend, the faster current runs to the outside of the bend. For most Class II water—almost by definition—the main current will be the best route. The absence of "white" water is not the determinant of the best channel; indeed, the standing waves created by the constriction of the main river current between obstacles, or by a narrowing of the riverbanks, is just the place to be. As long as these standing waves, or haystacks, created by the collision of the faster-moving waters of the main current with the slower waters at the bottom of the drop, are not of a magnitude to bury the bow of the canoe, it is better to put a few ladlefuls of water in the bow paddler's lap than to opt for the gravel bars or ledges at the sides.

Finding the Channel

Viewed from above, the inside of the bend may appear inviting in the absence of the unnerving splash of white water, but as canoers bear down on this "safer" channel, they may discover that there is insufficient water to get a canoe through, and the white that was not to be seen from above is now frothing at the base of a foot-and-a-half-high ledge. High water levels, on the other hand, may call for running the inside of the bend.

Often, you will be looking for a channel within a channel, but the principles are the same. If you look at the accompanying diagram you can visualize the "V," or tongue of water, which is created by a breach in an obstruction or by the force of water as it is constricted by two immovable obstacles.

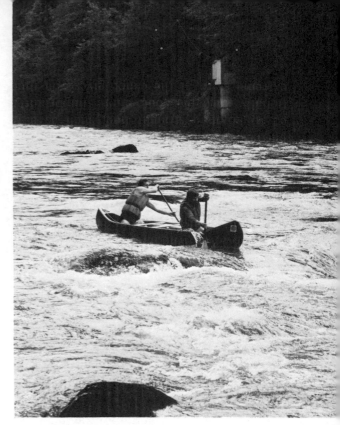

These paddlers head for the V or tongue of water between two obstructions. (Below) The V.

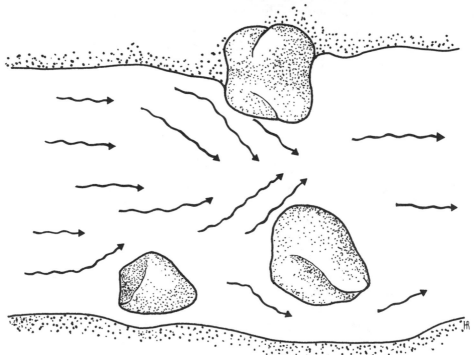

The Class III Rapid

If we add a few more obstructions to the diagram, we can create a Class III rapid, which by definition requires scouting and complex maneuvering. Additional geologic irregularities have interrupted the course and gradient of the river, so that the route is now in doubt. If gradient or water volume is increased, so is the degree of difficulty. A greater number of obstacles, or constrictions, cause the water to quicken or surge.

This new set of conditions calls for careful scouting. You should look for possible traps as well as escapes. You need to know where to go, how to get there, and what to do when you do get there; if you have any serious doubts, you shouldn't be there at all. Time to carry.

Class III water does have a route; it's just hard to find. The need to avoid rocks and boulders is obvious, but finding the inviting tongue (or "V") between two rocks, only to find a house-size boulder waiting at the bottom, can be discouraging. That's one trap. The other is the holes created by submerged boulders or ledges.

It is not the hole itself that is a problem; many small holes can be blasted through with hardly a bobble. The ones to be reckoned with are usually filled with foam that is more air than water and incapable of supporting the weight of boat and paddlers. The first casualty, as usual, is the bow paddler, who is buried as the diving bow keeps on diving. If the hole is not too large, and the paddlers can coordinate their braces and strong power strokes to pull themselves out of the hole, they may be only held up for a split second, take in a little water over the gunwales, and continue on. A more serious hole can eat a boat, holding it indefinitely and violently ejecting the paddlers from their craft.

Eddies

Needless to say, if there is any question about a set of rapids, avoid them. Aside from paddling techniques necessary for negotiating complex rapids, there are some escape hatches known as *eddies*.

You will find that behind each major obstruction or sharp corner there is a circulating current. That is the eddy current, and it is going upstream against the main current. Depending on the vigor of this circulation relative to the main downstream current, the eddy can be both a trap and an escape, but we'll discuss that in more detail later. For the time being, consider an eddy as a haven, a place to pull into for a rest while you scout the rest of the drop or reorganize your strategy.

RUNNING A CLASS III RAPID

Take the bow position in my canoe, and we will try to negotiate a complex section of water employing some of the strokes we have already learned on quieter waters, adding a few new techniques and strokes, dodging the traps and using the eddies. At first the channel is obvious as we follow the smooth tongue of water inclining downhill with deceptive smoothness. Then the narrowing of the channel and the ultimate collision with the quieter waters below combine to throw up a crosshatching of haystacks. We'll get a little wet but the channel is "clean," and our only strategy will be to stay mostly in line with the main force of the current and, if the waves are particularly heavy, to slow our momentum to minimize the rise and fall of our bow.

Standing Waves

As we near the bottom of the drop, we find that standing waves are piling up, creating higher peaks and deeper troughs. You have already learned the bracing stroke on the lake rollers, and you rotate your shoulders toward the gunwale, punching out with your lower hand—your paddle blade at a slight climbing angle to the water—and leaning on this stabilizing outrigger. As the canoe tops the crest of the next wave, threatening to spin us broadside, I quickly rotate my shoulders toward the water, reaching out with my paddle blade to catch a piece of the retreating wave. In fact, if I twist my torso far enough around and increase the angle of paddle bite, I can actually slow the canoe while maintaining stability.

As we reach the final climax of the drop, you decide that you're tired of taking water into your lap, and to slow the boat and minimize the slap into the final wave trough, you simply jam the paddle blade vertically into the water, prying up and forward and literally letting the boat down. We rest below, exhilarated by our rollercoaster ride and only a little wet.

Scouting from an Eddy

We now approach a bend to the right, but a house-sized boulder stands to the left of center just at the start of the bend, and the sharpness of the turn itself suggests that we need to stop and look the situation over. Just to our left is a low but unrunnable ledge, and just below that a protruding rock with a hole behind it. The main current is unmistakably to the far right, but we will not commit ourselves to the river before we have done some scouting.

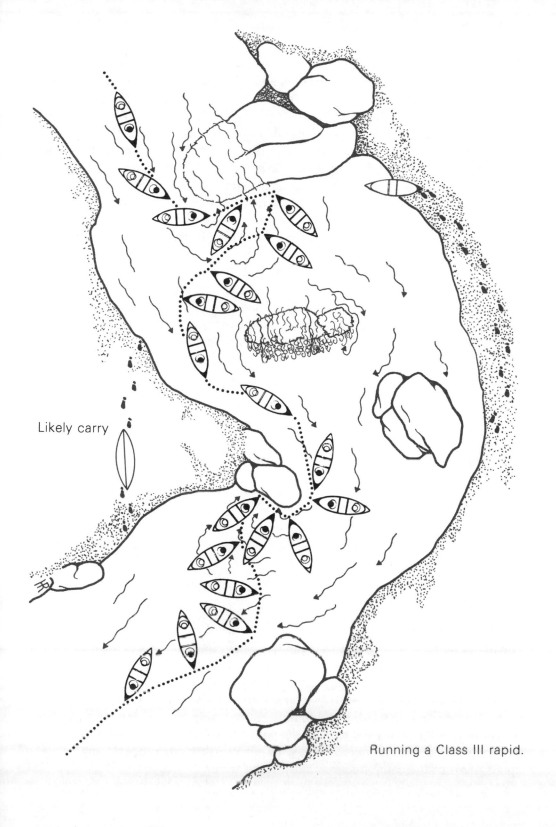

Likely carry

Running a Class III rapid.

Just behind the ledge on our left is a gently swirling eddy. Barely grazing the ledge with our left gunwale, we drive the bow of the canoe into its embrace. To do this, you start a draw stroke from your left-sided paddling position, making sure that you have crossed the eddy line and that you are planting your paddle into the eddy current, not the downstream current. You both draw and brace, putting your weight on the paddle blade and leaning hard to the inside of the turn. I am giving a hard sweep in the stern and leaning to the inside of the turn as well—but only after we cross the eddy line. The opposing direction of eddy and main current grab bow and stern respectively, actually whipping the boat around to face upstream. Since the bow draw is a power stroke—compared to my sweep and somewhat awkward lean to the side opposite my paddling side—you are in control for our eddy-in to the left.

Our reconnaissance reveals a clean channel to the far right, but we must be wary of being swept across and into the outside of the bend, where the water is piling up, to collide a little farther down with an unfriendly boulder. The river level is moderate to low, and we feel strong and confident.

Leaving the Eddy and Upstream Ferry

First we must extricate ourselves from the eddy and execute a short upstream ferry, to get ourselves across and above the rock and hole blocking the center of the channel. Below our first ledge, we are looking upstream, and now, with positive forward strokes, we drive the bow of the canoe across the eddy line and, maintaining a fine angle toward the opposite shore, allow the current to "ferry" us across. As soon as we have cleared the offending boulder and hole, you lean downstream, positively, and draw. Also leaning downstream, I sweep on the right as we come full around to point downriver. Oriented to the main body of the current, we both backpaddle slightly to slow ourselves and prepare for the next crucial move.

Eddying In

Just behind the jutting point which fills the inside of the bend is a boiling eddy. It will not be quite so forgiving of technique as our first one, so our strokes must be more precise and our lean, as we drop into the eddy, more positive. We have practiced our draws—including the cross draw—on calm water, and gone so far as to practice using a gently sloping shore or riverbank to get the feel of really leaning on our paddle. We found that by using hips, knees, and paddle we could heel the boat right over to the gunwale and bring it back up. Moving away from shore, we discovered that with our paddle blade properly angled we could perform the same maneuver using the water.

Current

A

B

C

Entering an Eddy
Paddlers drive across the eddy line into the eddy created by the boulder in the foreground (A). Using a stern sweep and bow draw (or high brace), both A and B show them leaning into the turn: they lost it momentarily in C and steady in D.

D

E

D

No time for reminiscing now! You rotate your torso fully from left to right, your upper elbow in tight against your ribs. Don't make a stroke; just get that blade into the water of the eddy immediately behind the point and lean on it as I pry hard on my right stern and lean hard to the right. The swirling currents of the eddy stop the canoe dead, but the rush of the river past the point punches the stern around. We are saved from being capsized only by our strong lean to the inside of the turn as we eddy in. So violent is our pivot that I must catch the careening stern with a low brace. Laying the nonpower face of the blade well out—and flat—on the water, I create a platform.

Eddying Out

We've made it. We give each other an encouraging word, compliment ourselves on a job well done. But our biggest challenge lies immediately ahead. With what is popularly known as a "peel-out," we must now get ourselves back across that violent eddy line, created by a powerful downstream current and its abrupt interruption by the point behind which we now rest—subdued but anticipating. By backing downstream somewhat, we can attack the eddy line a little farther down, where the demarcation is not so severe.

This upstream ferry starts as the paddlers drive their canoe across the eddy line into the main current (A). A strong pry (B, C) in the stern maintains the angle as the downstream current pushes the canoe across the river (C,D,E).

C

B

A

Getting into an eddy in heavy rapids requires more positive bracing and leaning into the turn. Note how far the bow paddler is out over the water.

Ready, we drive the bow out of the eddy. You hesitate for just a moment in the bow; your downstream lean and switch from left to right side for the cross draw is timorous—indecisive—like the downhill skier who instinctively leans toward the false security of the hill when the steep is suddenly intimidating. I try to compensate, but it is too late. In a twinkling, the downrushing current has pulled our upstream gunwale under, and we are going for a swim. Fortunately, the river empties into a quiet pool below, where we are able to quickly get ourselves and the boat to shore—our egos the only casualty.

Getting out of a strong eddy is one of the most difficult maneuvers in white-water canoeing, and for one of the partners there is an awkward lean downstream that must be made to the off side. When the off side happens to be the bow paddler's—as with our episode—the fact of the bow's being the first to face the torrent is even more critical. Only practice, and even getting wet, ultimately gives you the technique and the confidence to master the peel-out. The route to mastery is to practice these movements at every opportunity in modest eddies, exaggerating your execution and leans and working up a progression of difficulty.

Another way to eddy in. The stern paddler is lying on a low brace, leaning to the inside of the turn. The bow is using a bow pry as an alternate to the bow cross draw.

These paddlers are "peeling out" of an eddy, using a stern sweep and bow draw and high brace. Note their exaggerated lean downstream as they hit the main current and hold it until they are pointed straight downriver.

Role of the Bow Paddler

It's appropriate to comment here that the bow paddler's role in white water is crucial, and when the waters begin to rumble, the partner in the bow should become the captain. The bow is a better vantage point for reading the water, and the split-second advantage in decision making may be the difference between success and disaster. It is not unusual to see the stronger male partner in the bow, even among experienced male-female and husband-wife paddling teams, and including international competition. One enterprising instructor, who has given white-water clinics for years on the upper Hudson River, first puts the paddlers, many of whom are family members, into covered single canoes so that everyone learns both bow and stern strokes. It's a great idea.

The skills described up to this point will more than adequately equip you for both modest and ambitious adventures. Mastery of the strokes, and the gradual learning of the ways of moving waters, whether found on lakes or in the river valleys, should give you the confidence to tackle the sport of white water (described in the next chapter), canoe trips and the expeditions that grip your imagination.

LINING

There are times when a ledge or severe drop or a too-shallow riffle makes paddling dangerous or impractical. This is more of a problem for the canoe tripper who does not want to unload the canoe and make a portage (lining is described in more detail in chapter 9), but you may have occasion to line whenever you face such obstacles on a river.

By means of sturdy lines attached to bow and stern, the canoeing partners can alternately guide and restrain the canoe down and around offending obstacles. This can be managed from shore, but often requires the canoers to do some wading.

Here, a whitewater instructor gives lessons on the Potomac River, near Washington, D.C.

7

Canoeing for Sport

Beyond the basics of canoeing as transportation is the excitement of canoeing as a sport. Performance and skill mastery can be ends in themselves or can lead you into new and satisfying realms as a day cruiser, expedition paddler, or competitor. Performance canoeing usually means more boat time—the only way the skills can be developed—no matter what your athletic abilities may be. Sports physiologists know the benefits of "specificity of training." Simply put, if you want to run fast you have to practice running fast. In canoeing, the same principle applies.

Canoeing is often perceived as a non-athletic recreation, but as you get closer to some of the giants of sport—in Olympic flatwater paddling, in slalom and wildwater, or marathon racing—you discover athletes who are every bit as gifted and dedicated, and who put in the same long training hours as Florence Griffith-Joyner, Greg LeMond, Debi Thomas, and Dan Jansen. In canoeing their names include Lugbill, Hearn, Barton, Bellingham, Corbin, Phillips, and Newton. You need not aspire to their level of performance, but the skills they represent and the technology of the boats they paddle do trickle down to even the modestly aspiring paddler. You may never compete in a

Today's fast-cruising canoes are the paddler's equivalent of the cyclist's high performance bicycle.

canoe marathon or run the Grand Canyon, but you can find enhanced "motion pleasure" and higher return on your energy investment through the mastery of new skills and advanced boats.

Not for me, you say. But consider this. Even the once-a-year canoe tripper will be a safer, fitter, more efficient paddler, and derive more enjoyment from his trips if he practices and acquires advanced skills. To experience the best the sport has to offer, whether it is whitewater thrills, an expedition to a remote area, or a canoe triathlon, such skills are essential.

THE WORLD OF WHITEWATER

One can enjoy a lifetime of canoeing without ever essaying water more demanding than a class I river. For the canoe tripper, rapids are often the obstacle, something to be gotten around or through. The wilderness traveler will portage when there is the slightest doubt that the rapid can be safely run. But for the enthusiast, whitewater is the reason for paddling—not an obstacle, but the object. The true aficionado, can spend an entire day on a three mile section of his favorite whitewater run. He "plays" his way down the river, spending hours "surfing," "hole riding," peeling out, "endering," and performing a host of other maneuvers. He or she will endlessly analyze the dynamics and hydraulics of a drop to determine whether to run it, how to run it, and its potential for being played in. For some people, the point of running a whitewater stretch may be simply the adrenaline rush that comes from overcoming fear and finding control on a wildly plunging river. For others, the lure of hidden canyons requires that they master the boat and the skills. Still others undertake to learn the skills for heavy whitewater in preparation for an expedition to a remote area where the unexpected may require reflexive reactions in a tight spot.

THE BOATS

Not so long ago, the mastery of heavy whitewater, class IV and above, would have been considered the province solely of decked boats. The decked boats I refer to are technically C-1s and C-2s, and they look to the uninitiated like slightly plump kayaks. Like a kayak, they have a cockpit around which the paddler snaps a sprayskirt. Unlike a kayak there is a saddle for kneeling. Kneeling cups, toe blocks and thigh straps permit the decked C-1 paddler to exercise pinpoint control over his boat, even when performing the eskimo roll.

(Left) Thigh braces and knee pads provide better control to the white-water paddler. (Right) Performance-canoe design elements can be found in today's tripping canoes: sliding bucket seats, foot brace, sharp bow entry, and slightly asymmetrical hull.

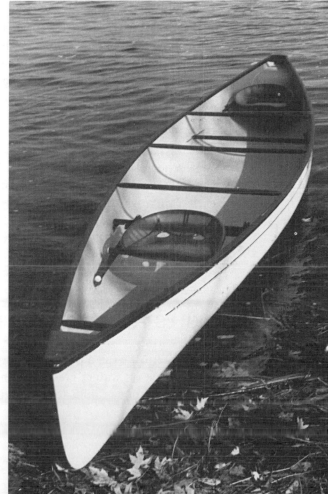

These boats are able to negotiate the biggest water runnable by kayaks and rafts, and recent dominance by Americans in world slalom racing competitions attests to the C-1's rising popularity here; ten years ago it was rare for an American to place even in the top 20.

Mastery of the C-1 may represent the ultimate whitewater canoeing skill. Few boats are as demanding or rewarding, and watching a skilled team of tandem paddlers in a C-2 is to witness an art. But the taming of heavy whitewater is no longer reserved to the decked C-1s and C-2s.

There have always been a few enthusiasts willing and able to tackle some pretty hairy stuff in their open canoes. The canoe was likely to be a beamy tripping canoe—maybe aluminum and, more recently, ABS—and home-outfitted with thwarts or saddles for kneeling, ethafoam blocks or innertubes for extra flotation, and partial decking. Most paddlers eschewed full-length, fabric decks for fear of getting stuck under them if their canoes capsized. Now, there are a host of open canoes for both solo and tandem canoers in ABS, polyethylene and Kevlar, which are specifically designed for high performance whitewater paddling. The boats generally have plenty of rocker for quick maneuvering, and most have some "flare" in the bow and carry their width well into the bow and stern to provide "lift" when plunging into the troughs and holes. The flare also retards plunging. Some whitewater open canoes are factory outfitted with bow and stern float bags, kneeling saddles, thigh braces, and knee pads, but most are sold with minimal outfitting, and the dealer installs custom accessories to make them ready for the river. These boats are as popular on Class II and Class III runs, but in skilled hands can be taken down almost any river capable of being run. Properly outfitted, they can be eskimo rolled (if one considers that to be a necessary skill), and in recent years groups of open canoers have paddled the full length of the Grand Canyon. Open whitewater canoe paddlers are now seen "playing" and performing the same maneuvers as their decked cousins.

In addition to specialized boat designs, today's serious whitewater canoer will carry a spare paddle, throwline, and bailer, and be clad in a wet suit or dry suit, helmet, and top quality PFD—one which provides the best combination of buoyancy and freedom of movement.

SKILLS FOR HEAVY WHITEWATER

In chapter 6 we ran a Class III rapid. That's no slouch. More whitewater action takes place on waters graded II and III than any other. Higher water levels, more continuous rapids (as distinguished from "pool and drop" river configu-

Fully-outfitted boat for whitewater. Note the sculptured kneeling saddle (with toe blocks) and flotation bags. This one is made of ABS with good rocker and a flared bow.

rations), or just plain anomalies, can put spine tingling challenge into a Class III rapid. Certainly, any river section of IV or higher would have to be considered heavy whitewater. Very low water can render even a Class IV drop impotent, in which case you might bump and scratch, but the dangers associated with heavy whitewater would be significantly reduced.

We will assume that we are talking now about full strength whitewater of Class III or better. This calls on all of the paddling skills discussed in earlier chapters, a few new ones, and certainly the more aggressive application of ones learned earlier. At a minimum, your lean downstream will be more exaggerated, your execution of strokes positive and vigorous. Draws and braces which were discussed in Chapter 6 must become second nature.

High and Low Braces

The braces must become almost instinctive, and that comes only with practice. The place to learn is on quiet water, perhaps a gently sloping shoreline. In winter, whitewater clubs often arrange for pool practice sessions. Whether in a pool or at the edge of a lake, you can practice extreme maneuvers, aggressively executed, with a minimum of discomfort when you go over the edge—and you should, or you're probably not trying hard enough. Canoes which are properly outfitted, preferably with knee pads and thigh braces, either open or decked, will permit you to gain maximum control over your boat.

The low brace, done on your paddle side, can be done in any quadrant (before, aft, or opposite your kneeling position), but initially you will want to learn to brace up with your paddle extended over the water perpendicular to the gunwale and just ahead of you. A trailing brace (aft quadrant), becomes the tool for surfing a wave face.

Using either a pool edge or the sloping bottom of a lake, practice rolling the canoe hull towards your paddle side. You want to roll your hips, not your upper torso; the object is to see how close you can bring the gunwale to the water. The reason for practicing on a sloping shore line is that your blade face (non-power side) can come to rest on the lake bottom, and you can practice snapping the boat back up with your hips without worrying about the water supporting you. Once you get the feel of the hip snap, which brings the boat back up without stressing arms and torso, you can move to deeper water. In a gunwale-to-the-water brace, your head will be over and close to the water, and your inside elbow close to your navel. Using the non-power face blade on the water as support, you push down on the paddle, snap your hips, and, *keeping your head close to the water,* bring the boat back up.

Practice, practice, practice. The best canoers will master bracing—up until it becomes, in effect, the final component of an eskimo roll. Easier than it sounds, in either a decked C-1 or a properly outfitted open canoe, the upside-down paddler must sweep his paddle into the low brace position while underwater, then brace up. This is a maneuver best learned in shallow water, from an experienced canoer, and one who can guide your paddle blade and right the canoe until the moves become second nature to you.

The low brace, practiced until it becomes instinctive, gets thrown out on the water whenever stability is threatened, and that can be when a canoe plunges over a river drop, drives into a boiling eddy, or when a twitchy racing canoe gets attacked by a power boat wake. As a kind of advanced survival skill, the low brace should be in every performance paddler's repetoire.

The low brace must become second nature to the whitewater canoer.

The high brace is a powerful stroke, like a draw in suspension. It is a must stroke in heavy whitewater.

The high brace is an even more athletic maneuver and can put the paddler into a position of leverage, well out over the water, where the boat can be kept in control in even the most horrendous conditions. For riding a hole or catching a wave, the high brace may be the only way to reach up and grab solid water. Think of the high brace as a draw stroke in dynamic suspension. Usually you will have the power face of your paddle blade planted well out from the boat, and the blade angle manipulated to compensate for the force and direction of the wave (the one you grabbed). The water's force will substitute for the in-drawing motion you learned on quieter waters. Put another way, in powerfully moving water, you convert the water's power to your use through the positioning of boat, body and paddle. Needless to say, this differs markedly from canoeing in non-moving water where the paddler must supply all the power.

The high brace can also be learned in a pool or at lake's edge. Blade angle—climbing in relation to the plane of the water—means the difference between finding support or a diving paddle blade; in the latter case you usually follow your blade into the water and go for a swim. As with the low brace, you must get your head and torso facing perpendicular to the gunwale, out over the water, and concentrate on using your hips and the thigh brace connection to control the boat hull. If practicing high or low braces gives you sore muscles for a week, you are probably overrelying on upper body and arm strength instead of proper body/boat orientation and hip snap. A face in the water (or as close as you can get), at both the start and the finish of a bracing manuever, usually indicates that you are using your hips and not your arms to brace up. That's good. Out on the river, the combination of instinctive braces and instinctive leans *downstream* will keep a canoe under control in even the most extreme conditions. Self-preservation is often dependent on doing that which seems instinctively intimidating, such as a downhill skier attacking a very steep hill by getting forward and away from the slope. If he succumbs to his ingrained fears and leans towards the mountain, he's a goner. Canoers must overcome a similar instinct. The upstream lean usually ends with a swim.

Cross Draw and Duffek

We discussed the cross draw in earlier chapters; like the draw, it becomes an off-side bracing stroke in heavy water. It's an awkward stoke for most people, and somewhat limited in its effectiveness. But it must be learned. We used it to eddy in on our Class III run in Chapter 6, and for peeling out when the direction of mean river current was coming at our paddling side as we left the eddy. Sometimes the hole rider will get swung to his offside (natural paddle side now facing upstream), and the agile canoer will manage to throw out a cross draw brace and a downstream lean to ride the downstream wave as it exits the hole. This may be the most difficult maneuver in canoeing—leaning downstream, away from your natural paddling side, and fully twisted to get your paddle and blade face on top of the water—without changing your paddle grip.

You may hear the term Duffek, and essentially it is a kayaker's stroke deriving its name from Czech slalom racer, Milo Duffek, who introduced it to the racing world 20 years ago. It is also called a "hanging draw" and a few other names, depending on local usage and the instructor. But whatever it is called, the principle is the same: Think of a kid running down the block and grabbing a passing light pole. The light pole doesn't budge, but the inertia of the runner almost lifts him off the ground and swings him violently around. The analagous paddler, rushing down river (into an eddy or around an obstruction), plants his paddle vertically in the water and with the blade oriented to "stand fast," the paddle acts as the light pole around which the canoe and paddler pivot smartly. Duffeks can be performed with hands high, hands low, close-in to the boat or away from the gunwale—often as a result of personal invention or the particulars of boat design. Both the cross draw and Duffek represent high attainment on the part of the canoer. One thousand pictures and one thousand practice grips and posturings on flat water, are no substitute for time on the river to develop the necessary "feel" for boat and water. As we shall see, even in performance canoeing on flat water, most well-executed paddle strokes do not involve the movement of paddle through water. The paddle blade is stationary in relation to its water-hold, and the paddler pulls his boat (or gunwale, or body, or bow, etc.) to the paddle. Alternatively, in whitewater, the force of the river provides the impetus around a firmly planted paddle blade.

FAST CRUISING

To the beginning paddler, the feel of slipping a lightly laden canoe across calm or dappled waters is a pleasure similar to the "free glide" savored by bikers and cross country skiers. Put a pack on the bike, on the skier's back or in the bottom of a canoe, and the return on the paddler/rider/skier's energy investment diminishes rapidly. After the initial pleasure of a free glide under optimal paddling conditions, one comes to appreciate the finer points of boat and paddle design and stroking techniques; they are a means of enhancing the pleasure and dealing with adverse, as opposed to optimal, conditions. And it's not just a

Fast-cruising canoes are quick and efficient—there's nothing like the feeling of gliding smoothly along calm waters at a brisk pace.

feeling of pleasure; you can measure the difference. With an efficient hull and good technique you can go 50 percent further on the same effort. Safety is enhanced, because a canoer can now sprint for a distant headland when an unexpected storm descends, and his energy level remains higher when conditions force him to paddle an additional six miles at the end of a long day. For the cruiser, efficiency means more time to enjoy the scene, cover more territory, and get the same satisfaction as the biker who has mastered a lightweight performance bicycle.

The Boats

Our "suitability chart" on page 31, stopped short of displaying actual hull dimensions, shape variations, and weight gradations under 75 pounds. The trickle down of technology in the form of advanced hull designs and materials available for recreational paddlers has accelerated in the past ten years, so that souped up designs may become the norm even for the fisherman who wants to get to his favorite fishing hole quicker.

CANOE magazine's annual "Buyer's Guide" lists over 1,000 hulls from almost 100 manufacturers. Asymmetrical hulls, formerly seen only on Olympic flatwater boats, downriver racing kayaks, and radical marathon racing canoes are now found in recreational hulls, even tripping boats. Simply, the widest point of the canoe at the waterline is aft of center, creating a longer, finer entry line; hence, less resistance. Asymetrical hulls, by design, will go faster and be more difficult to turn.

Asymmetry won't do it all. New construction methods, fabrics, and designs are bringing boats into the market which weigh 40 to 45 pounds for a tandem and 25 to 30 pounds for a solo—weights once found only in the most expensive racing machines. The degree of asymmetry, width at the gunwale, width at the widest point and width at the waterline will combine to determine a canoe's speed and the tradeoffs between maneuverability and stability. The fastest canoes will be difficult to turn and initially very unstable, requiring boat time and good stroking and bracing skills to get the most satisfaction from them. One does not need to go to the extreme designs to get the ultimate forward motion pleasure. Look at the dimensions for the so-called competition cruiser class of tandem boat as an example of a boat that most any recreational paddler can adapt to. While the dimensions of the competition cruiser are dictated by racing rules, the recreational adaptations may tack on additional depth, for example, to give a drier ride and more gear capacity. Such adaptations hardly detract from the potential hull speed.

A solo paddler seeking similar performance can find canoes weighing 40 pounds or less; one representative design for the performance paddler on flat water boasts an asymmetrical hull, is 16′ 8″ long, 22″ wide at the gunwale, 29″

Solo paddlers in Minnesota's Boundary Waters Canoe Area.

wide at the waterline, and is 12½" deep at the center. First introduced as a citizen racer's C-1, it soon became a popular solo touring boat. Confident canoe trippers have learned to take this and similar boats into the backcountry. As you might expect, the addition of a load to some of the tippier designs tends to increase the actual waterline width, lower the center of gravity, and give the paddler a more secure ride.

Performance Cruising Techniques

The paddle of choice for most of the performance cruising canoes is the bent shaft. You can brace, draw, pry, and even J-stroke with a bent shaft paddle— and it's worthwhile to have all of these strokes in your bag of tricks—but the essence of the fast cruiser's technique, adapted from marathon racing, is "hit and switch." Some call the technique "sit and switch," or the sit-down racing stroke. First of all, the stroke is effective because the performance canoes track well, requiring considerably fewer corrective strokes to keep them in fast forward. Second, the canoes are narrower at the gunwale, so that the paddler has only a short reach on either side of the canoe. Third, the bent shaft paddles are shorter and lighter, and easily swung from side to side. And when do you switch? In a hard-tracking solo canoe, the paddler may get three, four, and even five strokes on a side before switching, and in a tandem canoe paddlers could get as many as eight strokes on a side.

"Hit 'n switch" purists abhor any corrective stroke. Even though a switcher may appear to be zig-zagging down a course, it has been demonstrated that the prying or J-stroking paddler—though his course may appear to be straighter—is losing power and actually "crabbing" or sideslipping. Which leads to another corollary of the performance flatwater paddler. The paddle doesn't move through the water once the boat is moving up to hull speed; rather, the paddler is pulling himself to the paddle. Here's where the bent shaft delivers optimum performance: the blade is on a vertical plane throughout a greater portion of the forward stroke, meaning that the paddle holds its grip on the water longer.

The best flatwater paddlers transmit power to paddle through a smooth combination of stroke components: forward punch of upper shoulder, rotation of torso, and downward drive of the upper hand. There is a fast recovery and elliptical (feathered) return of the blade, whose insert on return is well forward of the paddler. During the power phase of the stroke, the paddle is close to the centerline or plane of the keel, and the paddler pushes his leg to full extension against the foot brace as the stroke is completed. Cadence might range from

40 strokes a minute for the casual, but fast-moving cruiser, to as many as 80 strokes per minute for a racer.

With the paddle switching sides so often, the switch itself is critical. In anticipation of the canoe veering off course, the paddler quickly switches to the other side, using his lower hand—at the end of the stroke—to put the paddle shaft into the opposite hand, keeping the blade up to clear the hull in front of him, and transferring the original lower hand to the top of the paddle grip on the new side. If you are paddling tandem, you must alert your bow partner of a side switch. The usual signal is "switch" or "hut" (the racer's term), and given at the start of the bow partner's stroke so that he can make the switch at its completion.

The fast cruiser will use, but infrequently, a low brace, draw, and cross draw. It is obvious that whitewater turbulence demands advanced techniques; it is less obvious that finely bred cruising hulls also require advanced techniques. For example, you might see the marathon canoe paddler use a form of Duffek, or "post," when trying to execute a turn. We associate the J-stroke with the Northwoods paddler or canoe tripper, but you'll find that stroke useful, too, when rough water and winds force you to get on one paddling side to counteract the hyper-weathervaning tendency of some of the twitchier hulls.

The braces are more likely to be used in surprise situations: the start of a race when the water erupts, or the sudden arrival of a motor boat wake. The hull that flies can be a bear to turn; you'll need a sweep stroke, a post, cross draw, and sometimes a combination. You will also need to learn to lean *away* from the direction of turn. That's because you have to get the cutting bow out of the water and use your tumblehome or waterline to create a bit of rocker. A typical turn to the left, for example, might involve reaching far forward and away from the canoe, sweeping the paddle in a broad arc and leaning well over on the paddling side. As the hull slows in its turn, you may need to reach across the hull with a cross bow draw (really more of a rudder) to complete the turn. An alternative which depends on forward momentum to initiate, more appropriate to the tandem crew, is for the bow paddler to insert a "post" in the water, while both paddlers lean to the outside of the turn and pivot around the post. The post is a paddle inserted vertically in the water, with the paddler's body twisted well towards the gunwale and the power face of the paddle *forward*. It's like a draw stroke cranked another 45 degrees towards the stern.

Described end-to-end, in all the jargon of the sport, performance paddling may sound intimidating. But keeping a performance bicycle upright and cruising, while worrying about cadence, wind, hills, gearing, body geometry, frame geometry, and circular pedal stroke, to say nothing of crazed or inattentive motorists, open sewer grates, broken glass, and marauding dogs sounds intimidating to the non-cyclist. I see a lot of people of very modest athletic ability or aspirations, who have mastered the performance bicycle, cruising effortless mile after mile—a hundred at a clip—and who think nothing of it. The good news for aspiring paddlers is that tipping over may get a little water up your nose, but your limbs will still be intact.

FREESTYLE CANOEING

Not everyone is interested in "going somewhere." I happen to like how a canoe helps me see more country, plumb the mystery canyon, penetrate the wilderness, get to the finish line, find the Indian ruins and fishing hole. But a number

The high brace. Not everyone is going somewhere.

of paddlers have found happiness in the Zen of paddling. The cult is dedicated enough to have developed a range of specialized boats and use postures, strokes, and maneuvers more akin to ballet than to the purposeful stride of us transportationists. They may kneel or sit, or affect the high kneel used by Olympic flatwater canoers). Broad-bladed paddles with carved grips maximize the paddler's control over the blade angle and pitch. Nicely manipulated strokes combined with carefully designed hulls permit the freestyle paddler to exercise total control over the boat. Extreme leans, pivots, and body manipulations relative to boat, paddle and water, remind one of the sort of body control exercised by the gymnast on a balance beam.

Freestyle canoeing also recognizes that we may not always have the time, opportunity or waterways to "go somewhere," and messing around in boats, as advised by the Rat in *The Wind in the Willows,* can be entirely satisfying. This is the concept of motion pleasure reduced to a micro-environment.

But, you ask, what's the quickest and most effective way to get grounded in freestyle, or any of the other forms of canoeing discussed in this chapter? Is it all trial and error, fumbling on one's own?

Mirabile dictu, in this day and age it doesn't have to be.

LEARNING THE ROPES

Like most people, I pedalled a bike for years thinking I knew how to cycle. Then I joined a cycling club—one with a real coach! In one year of group rides and training sessions I learned more about proper cycling technique, equipment and bike set-up than in all my previous years of biking. Soon, I was cycling at an 18 to 20 mph pace for rides of 40, 50 miles, and more. Until recently, finding clubs, instruction, much less coaching, has been difficult for canoers. Most top canoers had to learn their skills through trial and error, or were fortunate enough to find a mentor. Today, you can find not only canoe clubs, but specialized ones. My own city of Seattle has five canoeing/kayaking clubs that I am aware of. Some specialize in whitewater, including sea kayaking, tripping, and open whitewater canoeing, and one is primarily a racing club. CANOE magazine regularly advertises schools and camps for learning all facets of the sport. Today, no one should have to spend twenty-five years fumbling, as I did in both canoeing and cycling, to attain skills worthy of a sport. Finding a club or instructional group will not only speed your route to mastery—be it in whitewater, fast cruising, solo paddling, or freestyle—but you'll find compatible people and a high component of fun, as well.

Safety and Fitness

Is canoeing safe? A quick look at statistics is not comforting. Fear of the "tippy" canoe seems to be justified by the numbers of drownings associated with the craft—accidents usually involving hunters, fishermen, or other persons on a spur-of-the-moment canoe adventure. However, while canoes in the hands of the imprudent can be dangerous—like cars or guns—the *sport* of canoeing is safe. Boaters who enjoy canoeing in some organized fashion—canoe tripping, a club affiliation—and have received formal instruction are rarely the victims. As with driving fatalities, alcohol is a frequent accompaniment to canoe drownings, as is ignorance of basic safety practices. Ironically, the fewest fatalities have occurred in the heavy white-water branch of the sport, presumably because these participants have a healthy respect for the water and have equipped themselves with the necessary skills and protective gear.

KNOW THE WATER

It is worth repeating that boaters should have accurate foreknowledge of the waters they will be paddling and should be especially aware of possi-

A calculated risk—let good judgment be your guide whenever afloat.

ble changes in river levels and how such changes can affect the difficulty of the run. In many parts of the country, the water levels in popular rivers are monitored by the Forest Service, Department of Water Resources, or a similar agency to determine the flow rate, or level, often expressed in cubic feet per second (cfs). Supplementing these sources, boaters knowledgeable about a particular river can advise you what the cfs level means: for example, at 3,000 cfs this river is considered "squirrely" and demanding in the extreme, at 1,800 it is ideal, at 900 it becomes highly technical (meaning, lots of rocks to dodge), and below 600 there is not enough water to run it. Of course, knowing the cfs level without knowing the size of the watercourse or its gradient is about as useful as knowing the barometer reading without knowing whether it is rising or falling or which way the wind is blowing.

KNOW THE HAZARDS

Four basic canoeing hazards have killer potential: cold water, high water, sweepers, and reversals, the last three associated with moving water.

Cold Water

Depending on the season, cold water can be a problem anywhere, be it a local frog pond, a large lake, or a river. In some parts of the country, because of latitude or snowmelt (my own northwest rivers, for example), cold water is a hazard year round.

In cold water the normal human body loses heat thirty-two times faster than in air of comparable temperature, and life expectancy in 33- to 40-degree water can be as little as fifteen minutes. The danger is a condition called "hypothermia," which is the specific result of exposure to cold. Hypothermia usually follows the initial panic or shock of immersion, which literally takes away the breath, strains the heart, and quickly numbs the extremities. Signs of hypothermia are a subnormal temperature within the body core and the inability of the body to produce heat. The skin and nearby tissues cool fast, and the shutting down of peripheral circulation to the extremities causes heaviness and numbness. Survival depends on many variables, including water temperature and the victim's size, fat content, and activity. In advanced stages of hypothermia, unconsciousness develops as the core body temperature drops to 90 degrees Fahrenheit. When the temperature drops to 85 degrees, the heart fails.

High Water

High water is a potential hazard because it increases the river's power and, in addition, means cold water during spring runoff. Since the difficulty of rescue increases proportionately with the flow rate, boaters should always be aware of the possibility of a sudden rise in water levels, as a result of sun on snow pack, heavy rains, or a dam release.

Sweepers

Among experienced boaters, the hazard most feared and most capable of bringing all senses to full alert is the sweeper or strainer. This may be brush, a fallen tree, bridge pilings, or anything else that allows the water current to pass through but would pin the boater or boat to the obstacle. The water pressure in even a moderate current can be overwhelming to the entrapped person or boat, making rescue difficult if not impossible. The hazard is all the more insidious because of the lack of fanfare announcing its presence—unlike white water, which transmits obvious signals of potential danger. Scouting, local

Sweepers and strainers.

Holes.

Reversal.

knowledge, alertness, and total avoidance are the best defense. There are few rapids whose dangers can rival that of a seemingly innocuous tree recently toppled into a river by a spring storm.

Early-season runs present the greatest danger, owing to the high likelihood of storm-related debris and the lack of traffic. No boaters will be able to give you a scouting report. Of course, a storm at any time of year or sudden surges in water levels can put trees and roots into the river. Certain rivers may be prone to debris at any time, owing to heavy forest cover, unstable or loose soil, or consistent high volume of water flows. And certain river sections such as headwaters, braided channels in the lower sections (alluvial deposits and unstable soils), and the outsides of bends will also be more likely to contain sweepers. If a clear and obvious passage cannot be seen, at the first sign of a sweeper, boaters should pull into shore, scout the obstruction, and determine whether portaging, lining, or a cautious paddling route is called for.

For the very experienced boater, white-water obstacles, including reversals and holes, can provide good sport. But they can quickly become hazardous. The most dangerous reversals occur below weirs, or low dams—often deceptive because of the seemingly unimpressive drop—causing the surface water actually to be going upstream. This action can indefinitely trap a canoe or person between the drop and the reversal wave. In the most serious reversals or holes ("souse holes" in the extreme form), a swimmer's only hope may be to dive below the surface to find the current flowing downstream.

KNOW YOURSELVES

A realistic appraisal of your own physical and canoeing capabilities, in relation to the waters to be canoed, should keep you out of trouble. Being a good swimmer is no assurance of immunity and may well create a false sense of security. On the other hand, there is no reason why nonswimmers cannot actively pursue canoeing, unless they are nonswimmers because they fear the water. Being comfortable around water, knowing how to float or tread water, having faith in the buoyancy of both a swamped canoe and a life preserver, and being knowledgeable in other safety fundamentals can be adequate for the marginal swimmer.

One of the first rules of safe canoeing is never to canoe alone. On wilderness trips or on white water of Class II or above, three boats are a sensible minimum. Those who do canoe alone must be fully aware of the consequences and know themselves and their capabilities exceedingly well. In my experience, there are few who make the grade.

Knowing the boating capabilities of your companions is extremely important too. More than a few canoers have had to risk their own lives in an attempt to save another boater. The participation of marginal boaters in a given trip, be it one day or a month, depends on the composite skills of the group. In other words, one marginal boater in a party of ten strong ones would be acceptable, while two out of four is risky.

KNOW YOUR EQUIPMENT

Start with a safe boat, one that is equal to the water to be navigated and matched to your own skills. It should be sound of hull, buoyant, and free from sharp corners and projections such as nails, rivets, or bolts. Open white-water

A throw rope should be carried on river trips.

canoes should have extra flotation and although it is important to have bow and stern lines, these and other lines—in fact, anything that might cause entanglement when you come out of the boat, like a spray skirt that won't release or buckles or clothing that might catch or snag—need to be well stowed or secured. Also, canoe seats that are too low and hang onto the heels are uncomfortable and potentially dangerous.

C-1's should be fitted with a simple-to-release spray skirt, grab loops at least six inches in diameter on both bow and stern, and a stern painter seven to eight feet long, secured by a quick-releasing S hook of coat-hanger wire just behind the cockpit. Grab loops and painter provide the means for self-rescue as well as for the rescue of other boaters.

Another important safety accessory for white-water boaters is a throw rope, 15 to 25 feet long. Have it ready when suspected water is approached. In addition to being a potential lifeline to a swimmer, it can also be used to winch a boat off a boulder.

PFDs, or life preservers, were covered in chapter 2, but their importance to safe boating cannot be overemphasized. For club trips, the leader should carry basic first-aid supplies, and for longer trips a comprehensive kit, perhaps assembled with the help of a family doctor. Choose clothing either for protection from cold or against the sun and its reflected rays. Wool and pile are the best protection against cold water—even when wet—but a wet suit is a necessity for white-water boaters when water temperatures are in the sixties or below. Whether to choose a full-length or shorty wet suit, and of $1/8$ or $3/8$ inch thickness, will depend on the water and air temperatures expected—the heavier full suit gives more protection. Avoid nylon and cotton, which, when wet, act as a wick to carry heat away from the body.

Light shoes of some sort should be worn as protection both in and out of the boat, and in case of a white-water swim. For head protection, closed boaters require helmets; increasingly, open canoe white-water boaters are wearing them too.

TAKING CARE OF YOURSELF

Recreational canoeing on protected waters is not a strenuous sport. The physical motions of canoeing are natural, and every stroke is followed by a free glide. And even though canoe tripping requires you to be reasonably fit, it is possible to plan a trip's itinerary to work your way to fitness as the trip progresses. Most people return from a one- or two-week trip feeling harder and fitter than ever before in their lives.

For those of you who plan to do a lot of white-water boating or expedition canoeing, good physical conditioning is a must, not only to meet the emergencies but in order to increase your enjoyment of the sport. Serious racers, whether flat-water, downriver, or slalom, are in top physical condition. On an NBC Special, "The Fittest of Them All," three top U.S. kayakers competed against seven other "mountainmen"—runners and climbers—in an eight-event competition. The first- and second-place winners, Chuck Lyda and Tom Ruwitch, were kayakers, with Eric Evans, a former U.S. Team coach and perennial top finisher in international kayak competition, coming in sixth. The result was no surprise to kayakers and canoers familiar with the rigors of slalom racing.

(Evans, who has written several books on kayaking and is a regular contributor to outdoors magazines, is something of an evangelist on the subject of training, recommending a regimen of on-the-water and dry-land workouts, including weight training and aerobic exercises such as biking, running, and cross-country skiing. Most canoers are not going to need that degree of preparedness, but, as with paddling skills, your physical conditioning should be matched against the activity contemplated.)

Self-Preservation

Self-preservation and self-rescue need to be considered regardless of the level of canoeing challenge sought. Being around water is reason enough. To start with, prevention is always better than cure, so you can increase your odds by being a competent swimmer with the ability to handle yourself underwater. Always wear a PFD, keep your canoe in control, and be able to stop or reach shore before danger is encountered. Don't enter a rapid unless you are reasonably sure you can navigate it, and, in any event, be prepared to swim the entire rapid if you should go over.

A proper canoe has adequate buoyancy to support several people when fully swamped, so you should stay with your boat as long as it is practical. In a lake, if the distance from capsize to shore is beyond your swimming capability, stay with the boat. In a river you should also stay with the boat, unless you are putting yourself in even greater danger because of cold water or the approach of a violent rapid. Then get to shore or into an eddy as soon as possible. Whatever you do, hang onto your paddle! It will be hard to find, otherwise, and you will need it to get out.

Implicit in the success of any self-rescue strategy is not to panic. If you

HELP position.

are in open water with the water temperature suggesting the danger of hypo-thermia and the decision has already been made that shore is out of swimming reach, observe these procedures. Do not thrash around. The body loses the greatest amount of heat in the groin, armpits and sides, back of the neck, and head, and your clothing holds a certain amount of warm air (wool especially), providing flotation and protection. Exercise such as treading water causes the body to lose heat faster, so the trick is to keep still. Assuming you have a good buoyant PFD, you can climb back into the capsized boat or assume the fetal-like Heat Escape Lessening Posture (HELP), keeping as much of the head and neck above water as possible. Do not swim unless there is absolutely no chance of rescue and you are certain you can make it.

If you capsize in the rapids, stay *upstream* of the canoe and leave it only if it will improve your safety. Avoid the danger of being pinned between a swamped canoe and an obstacle such as a boulder. If forced to swim the rapids, go on your back, feet first, keeping your toes up. Never try standing up in fast water unless it is too shallow for swimming. Think of the same ferrying techniques used in paddling and watch for helpful eddies or slack water as you try to work your way toward shore. If you are not alone, one of your boating companions should try to get to you at the bottom of the drop, so that you can grab a painter or grab loop as he attempts to ferry you toward shore. This requires tremendous effort on the part of the rescuer—you will be dragging like a sea anchor—so try to help by kicking and swimming.

TAKING CARE OF OTHERS

The trickiest proposition in boating safety is knowing when to attempt a rescue, as well as what to do. Overly ambitious, or hasty, poorly conceived rescue attempts have often resulted in the rescuer's getting into trouble too. Attempts should be made from the safety of a boat by the strongest boater, or boaters, or preferably from shore, using an extended paddle or throwing line. Canoe clubs, camps, and training clinics teach canoe rescue techniques and how to deal with a swamped canoe, righting and emptying a canoe in both deep and shallow water, and techniques for extricating canoes trapped in fast water. It is worthwhile training, but only good judgment and experience should be your guide as to what constitutes a vain or self-endangering rescue attempt, be it of a boat or a boater.

A reality of white-water boating is that when a boater goes over in the rapids, there is no real possibility of rescue until boater and boat wash out at the bottom, and by then all that can go wrong will have gone wrong. So at the first opportunity for rescue, you must be ready to move quickly, using a throw line, or having a bow or stern line that the swimmer can grab. If a throw line is used from shore, it may be belayed around a tree or boulder.

You do not have to spend a lot of time in formal practice of rescue techniques unless you expect to spend a lot of time on white water, yet there are many opportunities to "play" with a capsized canoe to gain confidence in its buoyancy. Families, in particular, should spend some time in shallow, warm water, tipping the canoe over purposely, clambering in and out, making a game of seeing how many people it can support, and, finally, practicing emptying the canoe in deep and shallow water. The lesson is that aside from the techniques themselves a capsized canoe is no big deal. It happens. People do get wet. Just hang on to your canoe as if it were a big air mattress.

Throw line and tree belay.

Playing with a swamped canoe gives these kids confidence in their craft.

FIRST AID

We cannot give a full course in first aid here, but some basic know-how in certain water-related or outdoors situations should be covered. You might consider the following questions:

1. *What is the treatment for hypothermia?*

Since hypothermia is caused by exposure to cold, treatment is aimed at warming the victim from the inside out. Move the victim to shelter and warmth as rapidly as possible. Remove all wet clothes and apply heat to the central body core (no one ever died of cold hands or feet!) with hot water bottles or an electric blanket. In a remote situation, just putting a victim in a sleeping bag or wrapping in a blanket may not be sufficient, since, by definition, hypothermia victims are unable to generate their own heat. Thus an external source is necessary. An effective field measure is for one or two of the rescuers to remove their own clothing and use their own bodies to warm the victim's naked body. A sleeping bag or blanket should be used to conserve the body heat.

Wrong

Right

Avoiding entrapment.

If the victim appears dead, CPR*, including heart massage and mouth-to-mouth resuscitation, should be administered. All hypothermia victims should be seen by a doctor as soon as possible, since there are possible serious aftereffects associated with shock and the buildup of lactic acid in the system.

Unless conscious and able to take hot liquids, a victim should not be given anything to drink, especially not alcohol. The cold extremities should not be rubbed, as this merely diverts blood and heat away from the core. Do not wrap a hypothermic in a blanket without an auxiliary source of heat, unless it is for protection against further heat loss before treatment.

*Cardio-pulmonary resuscitation; the trip leader or some member of the canoeing party should have this training, especially on remote or difficult trips.

2. *Your canoe is suddenly being swept broadside into a log (sweeper). What should you do?*

Lean downstream—toward the log—and attempt to hurl yourself over the log. You want to avoid exposing your open hull to the current, and avoid having both you and your boat sucked under the log or tree, where limbs and branches might entrap you with their "strainer" effect.

3. *A canoeing accident has occurred on a local river. One of the victims appears to be without pulse or respiration when pulled from the water. What is the best method of artificial respiration, and how is it applied?*

The quickest and easiest method is mouth-to-mouth breathing and closed chest massage—CPR.

4. *While cooking dinner over a campfire, you accidentally pick up a hot spoon, burning your fingers. They are red and very sore. What now?*

Plunge them into cold water and hold them there until the burning stops and the pain lessens.

5. *You have finished your day's paddle and the takeout is a steep incline. You dislodge a rock which bounces down and hits your partner on the head. He falls and rolls a short distance. What should you do?*

Try not to move him until you determine the extent of his injuries. If he is conscious, inquire how he feels. Check for bleeding, breathing, and give first aid as required. If there is pallor and general weakness accompanied by a rapid pulse, the victim may be in shock. Nausea or vomiting may indicate a more severe case, and a cold and clammy body which goes into violent shaking with chattering teeth may indicate severe shock. In shock, heart and brain are suffering from a deficiency of blood, so place the victim in a near-horizontal position, feet slightly higher than head. In shock there is rapid loss of body heat, so the victim should be covered, top and bottom, with blankets or available garments. A little fluid (but no alcohol) may help if the victim is conscious. Beyond this, a doctor's treatment is called for. Transport to the hospital as soon as possible.

6. *Your child is fishing and suddenly cries out that he has a fish hook in his finger. What should you do?*

Push the hook through the skin completely; cut off the barb and pull out the hook. Flush the wound well with an antiseptic solution. Make sure tetanus shot is up to date.

Canoe Tripping

To many, canoe tripping is the sole reason for canoeing. A canoe trip provides challenge, relaxation, discovery, and the pleasure of a real-life adventure. There are still many unspoiled waterways; perhaps more rivers and wild areas will be set aside to be enjoyed by the self-propelled traveler. Many possibilities for canoe tripping also exist along populated waterways. A canoe trip may combine historical interest, physical challenge, and scenic beauty. Fishing, searching for wildlife, picture-taking, or just plain loafing are added attractions.

THE CREW

Canoe tripping may give you the camaraderie of summer camp, a satisfying wilderness experience with other men and women, or a more interdependent life-style for your family. Give a lot of thought to the makeup of your group. When you think about spending three days, a week, or a month seldom more than 17 feet away from your companions, you can see why your choice of crew is important.

To many, the canoe trip is the ultimate goal and the reward for attaining requisite skills.

On a canoe trip, the chemistry of you and your paddling partner is as important as the technical skills each of you know.

Slovenliness is certainly not what you're looking for in a canoeing companion, but too-great concern about being clean and freshly groomed can make for even more annoyance. If your prospective partner has a fussy palate, or a low tolerance for physical discomfort, think twice about spending your hard-earned vacation in his or her company. You may be even worse off with a macho type whose risk-taking can get you both into trouble. Happiness in canoe tripping is a judicious blend of adventuresomeness and good sense.

PLANNING THE TRIP

Assuming you have the necessary paddling skills for a trip and are fortunate enough to have convinced your family or some compatible comrades to join you, it's time to make plans. And planning, like getting there, can be half the fun.

Little steps and then big steps is the way to approach canoe tripping, especially if you are going to involve the family. The three-day trip with two overnights is a good warmer-upper; it's the time to find out if you know how to carry a canoe, if the tents and rain gear are watertight, if Susie is allergic to down or your hand-picked bow partner is scared of the dark. You need all the same gear—just less food—for a three-day trip as you do for two weeks, so it's perfect practice. And the penalty for leaving something behind will be only a temporary inconvenience.

Where to Go

Affiliation with a canoe club provides access to a source of ideas, as well as to scheduled trips organized by club members, but if you're a do-it-yourselfer, you have a project ahead. Your crew's proficiency and time are going to be your limiting factors. You will probably be looking for something within a reasonable traveling distance from home. The amount of time you plan to spend on your canoe trip should have some bearing on how much time is devoted to getting there. Driving fourteen hours to take a three-day trip is a waste of energy. Expedition planning is discussed in the next chapter; for now, let's look at the kinds of canoe trips for which there is readily available information, such as guidebooks or canoe maps, and organized facilities such as canoe rentals, designated campsites, or wilderness preserves, all or partially protected for canoeists. Moving clockwise around North America, such areas would include Algonquin Park in Ontario, the Boundary Waters Canoe Area (Quetico Park–Superior National Forest) shared by Ontario and Minnesota, the Allagash Wilderness Waterway in Maine, the Adirondack Preserve in New York, the Okefenokee Swamp in Florida and Georgia, the Buffalo National River in Arkansas, the National Scenic Riverways in the Ozarks, the Guadalupe in Texas, the John Day in Oregon, or the Upper Missouri in the Charles M. Russell National Wildlife Range in Montana, to name just a few.

For your first canoe trip, there is a lot to be said for heading to one of the more popular areas specifically designated for canoeing. There is comfort in having others around, and if you're taking little kids along, civilization nearby is reassuring.

Information Sources

A comprehensive listing of information sources for canoeing would fill an entire book. Fortunately, such a book exists. In an obvious labor of love, a librarian at Washington State University has compiled the most comprehensive up-to-date compendium on the subject ever published, *Wilderness Waterways: A Whole Water Reference for Paddlers*. I am sorry that over the years I have not had the benefit of such a volume—but perhaps I would have missed

There is a wealth of published information sources for the canoe tripper.

out on some of the fun involved in the time-consuming, often frustrating, occasionally revelatory quest for useful, pertinent information.

Usually canoe dealers or liveries will have a rack of materials, including waterway guides for the region they serve. Canoe clubs are another excellent source; in addition to their schedules of organized trips, many of these clubs publish regular newsletters containing trip reports.

Every state and province of Canada has the equivalent of a Department of Tourism, and a letter or phone call will bring forth a blizzard of freebies, from which may be culled some useful information. A better source seems to be state Departments of Fish and Game, Natural Resources, Lands and Forests, or Parks and Recreation.

Maps

Two excellent sources for maps are the United States Geological Survey, 12201 Sunrise Valley Drive, Reston, Virginia 22092, and the Canadian Map Office, 130 Bentley Avenue, Nepean, Ontario K2E 6T9, Canada. Both offer contour maps in a variety of scales but before ordering, you will need to obtain the indexes, specifying the scale (1:25,000, 1:50,000, 1:250,000, etc.), and/or state or province. These are provided at no charge and come with the map order forms.

Although the maps are quite detailed with respect to land contours and such geological features as swamps and glaciers, they often do not show recent road incursions or other development. So note the date of survey or revision. Also, they are not often accurate where rivers are concerned, depicting rapids that turn out to be nonexistent or totally ignoring a six-foot waterfall. However, a prospective route, once identified, can be researched through some of the other sources mentioned.

A more rational approach is to first identify a prospect from a guidebook or club source and then order the U.S.G.S. maps. For most of the waterways in the United States you will find the one-mile-to-the-inch (1:62,500) quadrangles to be most useful, whereas the more extensive regions of Canada are adequately displayed in the four-mile-to-the-inch (1:250,000) scale. A good number of the organized areas, such as the Boundary Waters Canoe Area or Algonquin Park, have special maps for the canoer, showing routes, portages, and even campsites.

Magazines

Magazines such as *Canoe & Kayak,* of course, cater specifically to the paddler; almost every issue contains an article about canoe tripping, somewhere in the world, and often a piece on waterways of a particular region or state. My favorite periodicals, in addition to *Canoe & Kayak,* include *Backpacker, National Geographic, Outside,* and *Sierra.*

And sometimes an inspiration is what you need. Years back, my wife and I happened to read Pierre Berton's spellbinding account of the greatest gold rush in history, *Klondike;* a year later our family launched two canoes on a tributary of the Yukon for a 500-mile journey to Dawson City.

In addition to the U.S.G.S. series, there are maps prepared especially for the canoeist.

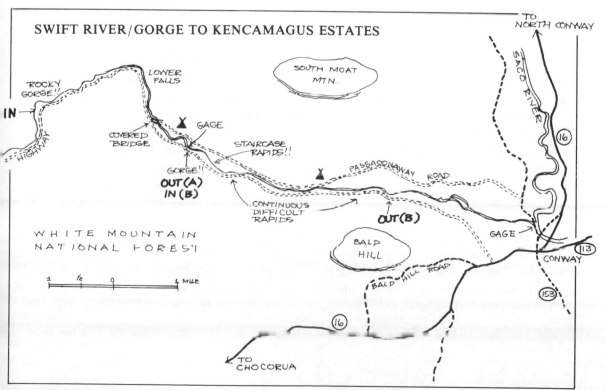

SWIFT RIVER/GORGE TO KENCAMAGUS ESTATES

When to Go

The traffic in popular canoeing areas can definitely detract from the solitude you seek, but peace and quiet can usually be found with a little ingenuity. Many times, research will reveal out-of-the-way access or egress points, and it may be well worth paying someone to shuttle you—perhaps by a motorboat tow—to get you and your crew off the overly beaten track. Even on popular routes it is possible to make short detours, up a side channel or around a corner into a secluded bay, where suddenly you are alone in your own little world.

Picking the time of year is very important too. Long-range weather predictions are hazardous, but one should have a reasonable idea of the weather patterns for the locale during the contemplated period of the trip. Having said that, consider trips before Memorial Day and after Labor Day; in both cases you are in and out before or after the bugs and people, and fishing is usually better early and late. July and August are the usual vacation months, so expect to find plenty of company, especially in organized canoeing areas. June before school lets out is a possibility, but in some parts of the Northeast it is the height of the blackfly season. Canoeing is full of compromises. I have taken canoe trips as early as April and as late as November. Any time can be great.

How to Go

Every year the roads reach farther into the backcountry. This has unfortunate implications, but it also means that there are very few canoe trips (as opposed to expeditions) that are not accessible by automobile. In the organized areas, some outfitters and other local entrepreneurs will provide a shuttle, using either your vehicle, or theirs, or both. In areas without such services, make inquiries at the gas station, general store, or local branch of government. Of course, if your complement of crew and canoes is going to require more than one car, you may have to organize your own shuttle.

How many people and canoes? Three canoes is a good number, each carrying two adults, which gives you a minimum safety margin in case one canoe should be lost or destroyed, but I wouldn't discourage parties of four, two, or even a solo from making plans. Just take the risks into consideration, and prepare and plan accordingly. If your party includes small kids or women, a good 17-foot tripping canoe can safely accomodate three persons. You may be a bit cramped, but sometimes it is the only solution.

As the crew grows in size, there is one unalterable truth: The larger the party, the slower it moves. Unless the group is experienced and extremely well organized, the likelihood of things going awry increases geometrically. A certain amount of tranquillity is sacrificed when a small navy embarks on a canoe trip, and I usually associate devastated campsites with their passing. On the other hand, a large group can be lots of fun. Some years ago, our family joined four other families and a dozen canoes for five days in the Adirondacks, managing to pack in a whole range of social and outdoor activities. We used the base-camp approach—in this case a large and comfortable campsite—so that those who wished to stay close to the hearth could do so. Others departed on fishing excursions, hikes, wildflower gathering, or mud-pie making.

The Trip Leader

What about a leader? From my experience, if a strong leader is called for, you probably have the wrong crew, and if you have to bludgeon any prospective member into helping plan the trip, you've got a problem before the paddles are wet. James Fenimore Cooper's Pathfinder was always referring to various persons' "gifts," and with good luck you may find a crew of leaders with a "gift" for each of the divisions of labor comprising the canoe-tripping experience: paddling, portering, tent raising, wood gathering, fireplace building, fishing, cooking, dishwashing, storytelling, and weather forecasting.

FOOD AND GEAR

If you enjoyed researching the "where" and "when," you're going to love planning the "what." As months turn to days and departure time nears, I make and remake my lists, organize and reorganize the menu. Despite having done this for twenty years, the fun endures. No matter how often you have been through it, you must have a complete list and then make sure every item is checked off as you pack it into the car. Many a canoe trip has found itself well downriver sans what one friend calls *le papier nécessaire*.

Durability and water repellence are the bywords for canoe-tripping gear. Weight is important but, except on the portage trail, it is far less critical than for the backpacker or biker. Canoeing equipment is subjected to rougher treatment: loaded and unloaded, stuffed and unstuffed, sat upon and mauled at canoe and campsite. The ultra-light gear of the backpacker has a short life expectancy on a canoe trip.

Canoes and Paddles

A good tripping canoe should be able to take abuse, weigh no more than 80 pounds, and be capable of carrying at least two full-sized paddlers and 300 pounds or more of food and gear. A center thwart rigged for a one-person carry with a paddle yoke or built-in yoke is a must. A good length of sturdy line in both bow and stern for lining, tracking, and securing is needed, as well as the usual sponge or bailer. A couple of sticks and perhaps the spare paddle on the bottom of the canoe will keep duffel off the floor, where the inevitable puddles eventually find their way through all but the most watertight packs.

Your paddles, which will end up being used as poles, levers, shovels, scythes, and filet boards, should be tough but light, so they don't feel like crowbars by day's end. A broken paddle can be a hassle, so in addition to choosing for durability, an extra for each canoe is good insurance. If you go with a synthetic paddle, some flex in the shaft is desirable. Avoid those with rubber coverings on the shaft—they are rough on the hands after several hours of paddling.

Packs and Packing

The theory in canoe packing is to consolidate as much as possible into a few very heavy packs, durable enough to survive the constant abrasions and concussions from getting them into and out of the canoe and which permit you to move all the gear across a portage, or from canoe to campsite, with the fewest number of trips.

Duluth packs (far left) or similar large, soft packs are preferred to frame packs by most canoe trippers.

Although one manufacturer has come up with a large-volume frame pack specifically designed for canoe tripping, most backpacks are too flimsy, too limited in capacity, and too restricted by a frame that is always in the way when you are trying to load the canoe. The ideal and traditional pack for tripping is still the Duluth pack, a giant envelope of heavy canvas, blessed with wide leather straps and, on the better models, a tumpline which allows you to support some of the weight with your head. In this way you can carry bulky, overweight loads for distances up to a mile, and, lined with heavy-duty garbage bags, doubled up, or with rubberized waterproof bags, your food and gear are well protected. One Duluth pack can carry two sleeping bags, sleeping mats, a tent, and an ax, and still have room to stuff the rain gear under the flap. Another pack can carry almost a week's food for a party of four. Depending on whether you are carrying gear or food, a Duluth may weigh from 45 to 125 pounds.

In addition to your workhorses, you will need some specialized packs, including one or more of the waterproof boxes or bags discussed in chapter 2. If there are kids in the crew, consider smaller packs that will not overload or endanger them. In fact, one manufacturer makes a nylon Duluth pack (a Klamath pack) with a plastic liner that weighs less than half the canvas ones. Duffel bags make good canoe packs and can either be fitted with a tumpline or stacked on top of another pack for a short stagger across a portage.

Very useful is a rigid, boxlike container, or "wanigan," which can carry daily implements such as pots and pans, utensils, a small tool kit, toilet paper, stove, matches, candles, file, and a few food items such as salt and pepper, plus the bread and makings for the next lunch stop. In short, it is a common repository for all the frequently needed cooking and camp items, so that once under way you will be able to avoid the dig-and-search routine.

To keep your gear dry, use a waterproof liner and see that the packs are slightly raised off the floor of the canoe. To preserve your low center of gravity, the weight needs to be concentrated toward the center of the canoe, with as little showing above the gunwale line as possible. Prudence also calls for tying or strapping in your gear, particularly if you're planning to run some rapids.

Clothing and Personal Gear

Most of what you need is probably already in your closet, and, exclusive of footwear, what you take should fit into a sleeping-bag-sized stuff bag. Plenty of socks are a must, ideally of wool or a wool blend. You'll need a regular change of socks and underwear, a couple of pairs of pants, an old work shirt, and perhaps a pair of shorts or swim trunks. If cool weather will be encountered, include a pile vest or a sweater. Wool or pile shirts or sweaters are preferred to cotton since both are warm even when wet. Synthetic fills such as Polartec and Fiberfill have pretty much replaced down, especially for wet environments. Pants of Supplex or fast-drying twills are superior to denim or corduroy. Wool or pile pants are a good choice for cold, wet environments.

Follow the layered approach to dressing; rather than wearing one heavy garment, don and doff several light shirts or sweaters, as temperatures and your level of activity require. Remember too that your PFD, topped by a windbreaker or rain shirt, acts as an effective insulator and substitute for a warm vest. The only other special items to consider are a hat, brimmed for wet weather or wool for cold; a couple of bandannas, for wiping everything from runny noses to knife blades; and a pair of work gloves. Old-timers swear by a change of socks. When you're cold, wet, or just plain fatigued, it's a great boost to the morale, and it really works.

Rain Gear

Without a doubt, rain gear is the single most important piece of clothing on a canoe trip. You can make do in lots of other areas, but why court misery? The old standby is the army poncho, which can also double as a tarp or ground cloth. It should have strong grommets at the corners and unfailing side snaps. Billowing over a fire, a poncho is a hazard around the campsite, so it should be belted or tied at the waist. It's nice to wrap your knees up in one as you paddle, but in the canoe it can become a sail-in-reverse when the wind blows. A poncho is also a bit ungainly if you are packing over a portage.

A full rain suit with a hood is definitely a much better choice. Be careful to avoid the extreme lightweight suits, which lack the durability required for the rough-and-tumble regimen of a canoe trip. Convenient but fragile, they most likely will end up leaking. A rain shirt with a minimum of zippers and snaps is also a good choice, or you may wish to pay top dollar for a quality rain jacket. There are many water-repellant, breathable suits on the market that give superb rain protection while producing a minimum of condensation. A popular brand is Gore-Tex.

Footwear

Many a canoe trip will incorporate some hiking, but hiking boots, as such, suffer a number of drawbacks as canoeing gear. Unless they are of the very lightweight variety, they are almost impossible to dry out in a reasonable amount of time. Resign yourself to the fact that your footwear is going to spend some time in the water. In ascending order of preference, one should consider inexpensive work boots, well oiled or treated for water repellence; waterproof boots such as Dunhams (very expensive); or rubber-bottomed 6- to 8-inch boots with leather uppers, such as Bean's Maine Hunting Shoe. The last are reasonably felt inexpensive, compared to a hiking boot, and come with a removable felt innersole that can be put into the bottom of your sleeping bag to dry at night.

Your boots will be fine around a rough campsite or on the portage trail, but for a change of shoes, an old pair of fast-drying tennis shoes is the answer. If the day's mileage calls for little rivers or scratchy rapids and the inevitable wading, these are the shoes. And, waiting dry in your pack, if you are fortunate, they are a pleasant change for evening around the camp.

Shelter

"Why live like a mole?" That was the rhetorical question years ago of a custom tentmaker who produced a unique tepeelike design in a little establishment under the el in upper Manhattan. He had a good point, and it is even truer today with the advent of versatile, lightweight fabrics for tents and rain flies.

Without the same weight constraints as the hiker, it makes sense to opt for the most spacious and rain-repellent shelter available. On a full-fledged expedition to the Northwest Territories, plagued by hordes of blackflies and mosquitoes which were tenacious beyond belief, we carried large six-person domes. In the evening our entire crew could escape inside with dinner, while the little devils pelted like raindrops against the nylon tent fabric.

There are more tent designs than we can adequately cover in this volume, but some general thoughts may be useful. Simple designs are best: A-frames, semi-wall, miner's tent, Baker, or the new Quonset and dome shapes, which set

A-frame, semi-wall, Quonset and dome designs make good canoe shelter.

up quickly with fiberglass wands and a minimum of guy lines. Look for models with small-gauge mosquito netting and lighter colors that tend to be more cheerful. The new lightweight tents usually come with an easy-to-erect rain fly and provide for adequate ventilation even if they are drenched by rain. Or you may do as we did, extending the life of our ten-year-old nylon A-frame by sewing a rain fly for it, using coated rip-stop nylon and a commercially available grommet kit.

Unless you are going to be sitting in a base camp, ease of setup and takedown is an important feature. Late in the day, as dusk gives way to darkness and rain clouds threaten, too much time spent with Tinker-Toy frames and tangled tent lines can be disheartening. Before you take off, set the tent up in the backyard, count all the tent stakes, guy lines, and poles, and check for torn grommets and decayed netting. Consider subjecting it to a summer thunderstorm to make sure it is going to keep you dry. If it's a new tent, this is the time to learn the idiosyncrasies of setup and takedown, rather than under the anxious eyes of a paddle-weary crew.

Sleeping Bags and Mats

Your choice of a fully cut, square-bottomed bag or a tubular mummy type is a matter of sleeping habits and preference, but the same comments made about tents concerning spaciousness versus weight considerations are applicable to bags. Choose either a high- or low-temperature rating, depending on where and during what season you plan to take your canoe trip. The size of your pocket-book may dictate the quality of construction, baffle-sewn being superior to sewn-through, and down-filled better than synthetic. A fine-quality down sleeping bag is a joy and delight forever, featuring maximum loft (which means more dead air space and consequent warmth) at the least weight and bulk. But down is expensive, somewhat fragile, and, if soaked, almost useless. I would tend to stay away from the cheap fillers. Consider, instead, the fine bags being made with Hollofil, Microloft, and Quallofil—trade names of the fiber manufactur-ers—for they are considerably less expensive than their down counterparts. They compress and stuff with a little more effort than down, and while there is a modest weight penalty (for equivalent warmth), they provide warmth even when wet and can withstand a lot of abuse.

Inflatable air mattresses mean comfort, and they can tame the most rugged terrain. However, an air mat of sufficiently heavy construction to resist punc-tures or midnight expiration carries a big weight penalty. Also, getting all the air out as you hurry to break camp in the morning can be a hassle, and in cold weather they conduct the cold.

Foam pads are a suitable alternative. They are warmer, and there is no need to worry about punctures. The most comfortable ones are about two inches thick, with an open-cell foam bonded to a thinner closed-cell layer, all encased in a nylon cover. Another ingenious new product is a self-inflating mat which combines the warmth of foam with the comfort of air and is proclaimed by some of my canoeing friends to be a true advancement in the state of the art of outdoor sleeping.

Camp and Kitchen Gear

Some of the organized canoeing areas are likely to restrict the cutting of firewood and firebuilding, and that's a shame, for the campfire is a traditional and integral part of canoe tripping. Unfortunately, that's the price we pay for years of abusing our wild areas.

In restricted areas, or where wood is just plain scarce, you will need to carry a stove. Fortunately, the popularity of backpacking has led to the development and refinement of a plethora of models which use a variety of fuels such as propane, kerosene, alcohol, and regular gas. Because of less worry about weight, canoers have a tendency to eat heartier than backpackers, so it is appropriate to shop for the more powerful, heavy-duty models. Two popular stoves are the Coleman Peak I and the MSR Whisperlite, both of which use liquid fuel. Be sure to carry the fuel in an absolutely leak-proof container designed for the purpose. As with the tents, a few practice sessions at home before you depart for the outback may spare you some anxious moments on the trail.

If you are fortunate enough to travel in an area where campfires are permitted, leave the stove at home. Even on heavily trafficked canoe routes, there is much drift- and downed wood to be found. This is especially true along the rivers. A small fire requiring less wood is environmentally smart, and much more efficient for cooking. Some organized areas already have fireplaces and grates in place; less developed routes will retain the handiwork of other travelers. It is wise to carry your own grill or fire irons, sturdy enough to support a four- to six-quart pot.

If there is an insufficient or improperly oriented windbreak, you may have to erect one. Some times a propped-up canoe is the ticket. In windy or rainy conditions you will need a windbreak for the stove as well, or the heat from your flame will be quickly dissipated—a great fuel waster.

For your fire, you will need tinder to light it, either manufactured (such as Hexamine tablets, candles, or waxed paper) or foraged, as well as tools for cutting and splitting firewood. A folding saw for cutting 18-inch logs and a small Hudson's Bay ax for splitting (hatchets are ineffective and dangerous) will do the trick nicely. Running the Middle Fork of the Salmon, we discovered that our saw and ax had been forgotten. There was a plentiful supply of driftwood, and we remedied our oversight by using soccer-ball-sized rocks to reduce the larger pieces to fireplace dimensions. This involved leaning the oversized limb against a rock and hurling our boulder down on it, making sure to get our toes out of the way.

Nesting pots and a juice container, accompanied by a spatula, serving spoon, and can opener, will comprise the cooking gear, and I suggest plastic bowls rather than the metal plates which usually come with cook kits. For grabbing hot pots, try a sturdy pair of goosenecked pliers instead of the unreliable handles that come with the nesting pots. They can serve a lot of other camp uses as well.

Depending on how strong a back you have or the number of portages you expect to encounter, there is a limitless amount of other paraphernalia you can tote along, from teddy bears to guitars. Radios and lanterns are incompatible with canoe tripping, but desirable options would include fishing equipment, a camera, and, for wind- or rain-bound camps, a deck of cards or paperback book. Binoculars seem to make sense but end up rarely being used. Flashlights, like lanterns, create a dependency, but are not of great value. They add weight and are superfluous during the summer when daylight comes at 4:30 A.M. and stays until 9 or 10 at night. A small spiral notepad and ballpoint pen are inexpensive, and if you are diligent in recording the day's events you will cherish the recall of otherwise forgotten details—the happenings and misadventures that are all part of the canoe-tripping experience.

Food

Canoe trippers travel on their stomachs. The length of the canoe trip and the degree of difficulty (usually measured by the number of portages!) will determine the type of camp kitchen and food you will carry. On one month-long trip down a swift but unobstructed river, we went 500 miles without a portage. Although we carried a great many freeze-dried meals, we were able to add canned goods and condiments, as weight was not the primary consideration. It's nice to be able to produce something extravagant for dinner after weeks of eating dehydrated fare.

For a weekend or short trip, anything goes, from ice chests full of steaks to a spartan diet of dried fruit and nuts. Where to buy the food? The grocery store has it all: everything from canned bacon, instant milk, oatmeal, dried fruit, and soup to packaged dinners, "helpers," and such standbys as Kraft or Chef Boy-ar-dee spaghetti and meat sauce.

For a longer trip dictating foods of less weight and bulk, consider light-weight prepackaged foods, dehydrated or freeze dried. There are several names to choose from, including Mountain House, Backpacker's Pantry, AlpineAire, and Richmoor. By ordering in quantity and then repacking the food in single-meal units, you can lower per-serving costs. Mountain House, for example, packages a full line of excellent freeze-dried food in No. 10 cans. The price is still high but not as bad as the meal-sized pack. If you need just a few lightweight meals, your local sporting goods store can probably supply your needs.

Be organized when you pack your grub. The supermarket staples, including dried milk, oatmeal, Tang, rice, instant mashed potatoes, coffee, and sugar, should be removed from their boxes, bags, or bottles and repackaged in double or triple Baggies (or Ziploc bags), put into a cloth bag, and labeled with Magic Marker. Tubes or plastic bottles are available from most backpacking suppliers, and into these go peanut butter, honey, and catsup. If there is more than one boat in your group, be sure to divide the food evenly between the boats, with approximately equal days' meals in each.

You may find the consistency and flavor of trail foods somewhat bland and uniform, although they have improved tremendously in the past few years. Consequently, you might spice up your food pack with seasonings such as onion flakes, bell peppers, parsley, curry powder, bouillon cubes, salt and pepper—in fact, anything you like to use at home.

Store-bought bread tends to crush and crumble, if it survives the midnight raids of the squirrels and raccoons. One answer is bannock or trail bread. Ingredients are all measured and premixed at home and packed in plastic bags. Pull out a bag and add just enough water to make a kneadable blob. Mix this in the bag and spread the blob in a frying pan for over-the-fire cooking or in a loaf pan for reflector-oven baking. When using a frypan, just prop the pan in front of the fire, after the bottom is done, and bake until the top is golden brown.

Canoe Trail Ecology

How do you clean up the mess? Pam sprayed on the inside of pots and pans before use helps them come clean. For general dishwashing, we heat water in the biggest pot, add some dish soap (biodegradables for campers are available), then rinse well and dry. For larger groups on an outing of a week or more, it would be a wise precaution to boil all the silverware, cups, and dishes (without soap) periodically.

S.O.S. can be used for heavy scouring, but don't be too concerned about getting all the black off the pots. Use the plastic bag that the last meal was packed in to cover the pot before it is nested up.

This leads us into the subject of canoe trail ecology. Too many people, too much garbage, too much soapsuds: It all adds up. Where there is an abundance of moving water, your cleaning activities are quickly flushed into oblivion if you are using biodegradable soaps. In heavily trafficked areas and on smaller waterways, one needs to be more attentive to the potential for polluting. That which can be burned should be burned. A small pit lined with stones can serve as your "drain field" for the dirty dishwater. In any case, that which cannot be burned, or flushed should be packed up and carried out. In many organized areas, plastic bags are provided (and even registered); the park overseers want to see them brought out full! We have traveled in some areas where these rules are stringently enforced—in one such area, fires must be built on a pan and the ashes carried out—and it's worth the effort. It seems a pity that bureaucratic rules have to be imposed on otherwise carefree outdoor pursuits, but the benefit is clean and appealing campsites where we can nurture the illusion, if not the reality, that we are their "discoverers."

Carrying out what you carry in doesn't apply only to your tin cans and soapsuds, either. A discarded tennis shoe, broken Styrofoam ice chest, or punctured air mat is just as unsightly as an empty Dinty Moore Beef Stew can. "Take only pictures, leave only footprints," is an overworn entreaty, but worth repeating.

What people take is almost as insidious as what they leave. Stripping the bark from trees, appropriating signs, privy doors, fire grates, and other public conveniences, is thoughtless and unnecessary. The Golden Rule is applicable here: Thoughtful canoe campers will leave a campsite in the same tidy condition that they would want to find after a good day's paddle, even if it means picking up after a sloppy predecessor.

Drinking Water

Running water in sunlight purifies very quickly, but there are only a few remote areas in the North where you can dip your cup into a lake or stream and feel confident that the water is safe to drink. Treating your water is good insurance against waterborne "critters" and toxins. Boiling water or using Iodine tablets have been the time-honored fixes, but you'll get better tasting water by using a purifier. There are many excellent, lightweight, and portable models on the market.

Assuming you have chosen an area and obtained good maps, it is time to plan the route. The critical factors, in addition to the proficiency of the crew, are total mileage, size and orientation of the lakes, number of portages (known and unknown), river gradients and obstacles such as falls, rapids, or dams that may have to be scouted, and, finally, the purpose of the trip itself. If relaxation and enjoyment of the fishing or scenery along the way is the goal, your mileage allowance will, of course, be conservative.

The Strategy

A family group traveling through little lakes and streams, with a portage each day, may plan no more than 7 to 10 miles per day and allow for several layovers or rest days. A red-blooded group of men or women planning to descend a reasonably challenging river with known and unknown obstacles might consider 15 to 30 miles a day; any rest day would merely be a dividend paid for overachieving one day's anticipated mileage. Then, there are big rivers with gradient and few obstacles, where a five- to eight-mph current lets a canoeing party knock off 30 to 50 miles in a long day. After you have considered all the factors, add in some insurance, in any case.

In addition to your maps, you may consult with earlier parties, local sportsmen, or, in the case of organized areas, one of the outfitters. These sources should help you in marking out a route, including the nature and location of campsites, the likely and known obstacles or dangers on a particular river, the length, location, and condition of the portage trails, and the effect of present or recent water levels along your proposed route. Two months of rain, or an enterprising beaver, can significantly alter a water trail from that shown on the map. The most important thing to remember, however, is that after you have gathered all the best available advice, look upon it only as a clue. Even the most knowledgeable people, although desiring to be helpful, have memory blanks, or perceptions that would differ greatly from your own (or another expert's); in the final analysis, you must rely on yourself.

Prior to your mileage considerations, you may have to make some other strategy decisions, often dictated by the geography itself. A canoe trip can go point-to-point, such as a downriver trip; in a circle, which also maximizes the variety of scene while avoiding the need of a shuttle; or perhaps a partial circle, which may retrace part of the outbound route. One strategy, which may be particularly suited to a first time or family crew, is the base camp trip mentioned earlier. Here one seeks to find a large, comfortable site, offering as many indigenous attractions as possible, while permitting one-day or overnight excursions on foot or by canoe. The establishment of a well-organized and comfortable base permits more sedentary members of the group to read, swim, sunbathe, carve, or just putter while others take off on hiking, fishing, spelunking, photography, or white-water excursions. The peripatetic ones can return to a base which, with each passing day, becomes more comfortable.

The Canoe Route

Traveling downriver, the problem obviously will not be one of "finding one's way" but, rather, knowing the location and severity of obstacles and when and where to get off the river to scout or to portage. You will also need to know the location of campsites and perhaps fresh water. If heavy rapids or a falls are to be encountered, you need to mark your map and know beforehand the landmarks that signal their imminence. These might include a noticeable elbow in the river's course, a tributary, an abandoned cabin, or a prominent outcropping of rock. Often a portage trail will commence even before the falls, rapid, or sharp bend can be seen. On well-traveled routes, these portages are likely to be clearly marked, but as one gets farther and farther from civilization, the signs may become more obscure and the penalty for a miscalculation more severe.

In the case of waterfalls, you had better have a good idea beforehand of the location of the portage.

Careful scouting of an otherwise questionable rapid may suggest several strategies, including the avoidance of a laborious portage. By carrying just the gear around the drop, your canoe is lightened and more maneuverable, and you have eliminated the risk of losing food and duffel. Then it is possible that two of your crew, considerably more skilled than the others, can paddle all the canoes through, to rendezvous with the rest of the crew at the bottom of the drop. For years, this was the strategy my wife and I employed with our young kids.

Lining

Still another strategy, which is one of canoe tripping's most endearing techniques, is known as lining. Sometimes it just means wading and hauling the canoe through the shallower pools and drops at the perimeter of a rapid. In its purest form, lining consists of people at bow and stern, alternately pulling and yielding on lines attached to bow and stern, letting their loaded or unloaded canoe down a drop deemed otherwise unrunnable. Clarity of communication between partners and an understanding of the physics of water, boat, and line are absolutely essential to the success of the operation. Should the canoe be allowed to get broadside to the current, due to inattentiveness at the stern or

"Lining" a canoe often ends up as an exercise in wading.

Following the route. Stay on the downward side
of the islands to gain protection from the wind.

excessive hauling in at the bow, catastrophe can only be averted by immediately
letting go of the stern line so that the canoe swings full around as the person
at the bow continues to hang on for dear life. Lining is often impractical where
there is a torturous shoreline, requiring the paddlers to go into the water up
to their waists or higher, sometimes hanging onto the canoe, sometimes using
the lines to restrain it.

Other Navigation Problems

On a many-channeled river, you may have to choose the proper channel. It is
often not self-evident, but try to take the first and largest channel in terms of
volume. Often a wide but shallow channel will beckon promisingly, only to
peter out noisily through a gravel bar at the lower end of a midriver island.

200-yard portage

Good humor is apt to be your ultimate salvation in any of these situations.

Finding your way down a sizable lake to locate either a stream outlet or portage presents different problems. Also, the presence or threat of wind or storm will affect your strategy. The navigational challenge is one of translating the two-dimensional map to a three-dimensional reality, seen from the constantly changing vantage point of the canoer. It's not as difficult as it sounds.

Using Your Map

As you move north to south on the map, you will be counting off the reference points, your map spread out before you on the packs. An occasional check of the compass will keep you oriented, as you attain each "headland" or island. These reference points, in addition to deep bays or a prominent contour (perhaps a cliff or peak jutting above the surrounding topography), are constantly checked back against the map, as you strain to pick out the next distant headland. Although your course as the crow flies may lie directly to the south, a route designed to avoid the wind, by seeking the lee protection of points or islands, may take you on the zigzag course shown on the map. Attentiveness, rather than sophisticated navigation, will usually ensure success.

Your outlet is likely to be found in the obvious topographic depression discernible at the south end of the lake. The higher ground skirting the marshy outlet of an intermittent creek is the likely location of your portage. A weathered blaze on an old tree trunk and a grassy clearing trampled down by earlier parties are evidence that you have found it.

The Portage Trail

The portage is much maligned, and unfairly so. It is work, to be sure, but the reward is a change of scene and new vistas. After several hours of paddling, the prospect of stretching the legs mingles with the anticipation of glimpsing a new body of water at trail's end. Too, several portages are likely to put you beyond the throngs of weekend paddlers. Indeed, it is the portage trail that makes possible a long and varied canoe trip carrying you across the watersheds, through the forest, and around falls and unrunnable rapids.

Being organized and knowing how to negotiate a portage can prevent an ordeal. If you know your route involves many portages, pack accordingly; more freeze-dried and lightweight food, fewer but larger packs, fewer changes of clothes, tents and bedding selected for lightness, and, most importantly, canoes no heavier than 75 pounds with a suitable yoke. Be stingy with the miscellaneous items. Count up the number of loads or packs (some may be carried two at a time), plus the canoes, and divide by the number in your crew. If the answer is more than two, try harder. Doubling a portage—that's two trips for one or more of the party—is fine, but if the portages are long or numerous, making three trips is laborious and time-consuming.

At the start of the portage trail, those with the heaviest packs, or the canoes, should be given some assistance. All loose gear should be consolidated to eliminate anyone's having to carry packs, tackle boxes, or cook pots in their hands. Paddles, if they are not being used as part of the carrying yoke, can be used as hiking staffs. Other than the bow and stern lines, try to refrain from stuffing odds and ends into the ends of the canoe; you'll upset the balance and exaggerate the weight (the lever principle again). If it's bug season, apply bug dope before you wed yourself to pack or canoe and head off down the trail.

Depending on the amount of traffic and the terrain, portages run the gamut

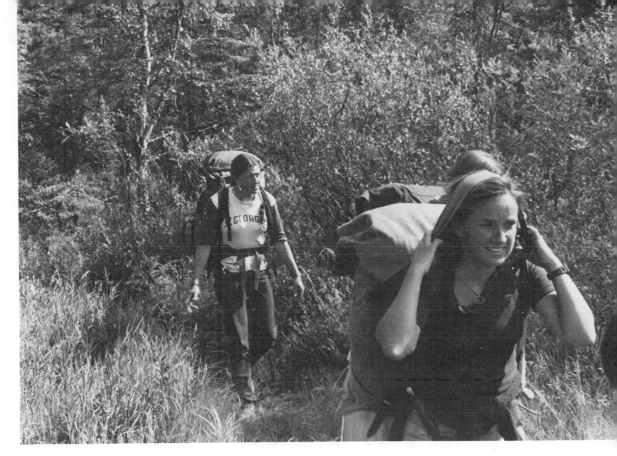

The portage trail is a part of canoe tripping.

from forest path to rocky staircase and gooey quagmire, sometimes all three on the same trail. It is often wise to test the length and condition of the trail with one of the lighter loads before staggering off with the canoe over your eyes. Once started, a good rule to follow is to "step over," not "on," rocks and logs.

Rest as frequently as need be. Another strategy is to carry one pack halfway across and then return for your second load, the return walk serving as a rest. The canoe carrier should be on the lookout for a friendly tree crotch —perhaps identified on the first trip—where the bow of the canoe can be wedged for a rest stop, without having to go through the much more strenuous exercise of getting the canoe up and down from the shoulders.

Perhaps the most important tactic on the portage trail is the encouraging word. A white lie, now and then, is permissible. "Keep moving, Dave. You're almost there." It's enough to keep you going, and there are few sensations to compare with that first glimpse of blue water as trail's end is neared.

Finding and Choosing a Campsite

Campsites are either a result of planning or a refuge of expediency. The latter usually represents a plan gone awry. The intended campsite was no doubt chosen because its location coincided with your mileage-per-day estimates, a rumored fishing hole, the outfitter or diarist's glowing description, or because it was the last piece of dry ground before the route vanished into ten miles of swamp. One of the predictable things in canoe tripping is that trips seldom unfold as planned, but if predictability were your objective you would have stayed home and watched baseball. Thus, it should not unravel you when a windy lake, a wrong turn, or a balky crew prevents your party from achieving the planned mileage, meaning you will be searching for a bivouac of expediency.

Even if you reach the intended objective, it is possible that it will be occupied. Depending on the desperateness of the situation, the condition of your crew, and the lateness of the hour, you must decide whether or not to impose yourself—if the site can accommodate another party—sweat out the next ten miles, or backtrack to an undesirable but adequate site.

If you have no predetermined camps, be aware of another law of canoe tripping: The later the hour and the more tired the crew, the fussier they become in choosing a campsite. Start looking early—say around 3 P.M.—and if you see one that meets your basic needs, grab it. A lot of campsites of expediency have resulted from ignoring this law. Sometimes, it will be uncooperative Mother Nature that forces choice upon you. How often the wind has driven us to seek the nearest refuge, to make do, until the weather decided to release us.

Assuming you have a choice, what should you be looking for? Perfection is a breezy, bug-free point blessed by morning and evening sun and yet not so exposed as to be at the mercy of inclement weather. It is gently sloped to shed a heavy rain, high enough above the water so as not to be drowned in chill morning mists rising off the water, and of even disposition for the setting of tents and mats. Its ample open area provides a view and feeling of freedom while, nearby, a fine forest exudes wilderness and yields plenty of dry wood. Earlier canoers will have built an unobtrusive but utilitarian fireplace and left a small stack of dry wood for the next campers—you. That, in fact, will be the only evidence of their passing through.

A sandy beach or drop-off will invite you to swim or fish. Fresh water will be easily accessible from the camp kitchen. As evening falls, the haunting cry of the loon and the rising drone of night sounds will slowly envelop you and your companions. As the final embers of your campfire expire, one by one, your exhausted crew will retire to the warmth and security of their tents.

Finding the perfect campsite after a long day's paddle.

A gravel bar makes a fine campsite.

That's the way it is—sometimes. Often you will have to compromise. But perfection means different things to different people. The tantalizing rapids that promise great fishing to one member of the crew may be a noisy reminder to another, who tosses and turns throughout the night, knowing that in the morning they must be run. But the search for Shangri-la is one of the joys of canoe tripping, and memorable campsites are often the plot in the unfolding story, the paddling and portaging only a means to an end.

The following checklist is time-tested, but each person has different ideas about what's a necessity, so the list will be expanded or contracted depending on the individual. The important thing is to make a final check of your list and your outfit before you launch into the wilderness.

Canoe Trip Checklist

Clothing

__full-brimmed or wool hat
__work gloves
__boots, waterproof or rubber-bottomed
__wool socks (or wool blend)
__denim or khaki long pants (one change)
__hiking shorts
__wool shirt
__pile vest
__rain suit or poncho
__underwear
__bandannas or handkerchiefs
__towel
__tennis shoes

Tents and Bedding

—tent with rain fly
—extra rain tarp
—sash cord or nylon line (for rigging rain tarps, etc.)
—down, PolarGuard, or Fiberfill sleeping bag
—foam mats (or air/foam such as Therma-Rest)

—nesting pots and pans with cups
—plastic bowls
—two-quart juice container
—knives, forks, spoons
—soup and coffee ladle
—large spoon
—spatula
—foil
—paper towels
—S.O.S. or Tuffy
—toilet paper
—stove
—candles or fire starter
—sharp heavy-duty knife
—tools (including goose-necked pliers for grabbing pots)
—folding saw and Hudson's Bay ax
—matches (in match safe or waterproof container)

Canoe Equipment

—paddles (one extra for each canoe)
—PFDs
—bailer and sponge
—heavy line for lining, securing, throw rope
—maps, trip notes, and waterproof case
—compass

Miscellaneous

—insect repellent
—biodegradable soap
—bug spray
—fishing rods and tackle
—camera and film
—paperback book
—notebook and pen
—shaving kit

10

The Expedition

As recently as 1904, magazine writer Leonidas Hubbard and his companion, Dillon Wallace, a New York lawyer, dreamed of exploring by canoe the *terra incognita* of Labrador. Their trip came to pass, only to end in nightmare and the death by starvation of young Hubbard.

But today there are no blank spaces on the map of North America—or anywhere else, for that matter. Even those remote places touched only briefly by the explorer's foot have yielded to the satellite's searching eye or the geologist's magnetometer. Atavistic yearnings cause us to ponder the map and the possibilities, nonetheless. For some, a four-day canoe trip in the Ozarks of Missouri will satisfy the hunger. Others need longer canoe trips, to more remote places, until, one day, succumbing to the urge to test the limits of their outdoor and canoeing skills.

Despite civilization's pervasiveness, places still exist where the illusion, if not the actuality, of total aloneness can be experienced. Another kind of trip might touch inhabited areas in many places, but be of such duration and complexity— for example, crossing a continent—as to be, in every sense, an expedition.

The canoe expeditioner cuts the cord to so-

Large lakes require that the expeditioner be able to translate on a grand scale.

called creature comforts to pursue self-reliance, dreaming, researching, planning; finally bringing people, canoes, food, and gear together for a trip that, one hopes, will fall just short of being an "adventure" of the sort that arctic explorer Vilhjalmur Stefansson called a sign of bad planning.

SKILLS

The requisites for a canoe expedition are imagination, curiosity, and skills to match. Beyond that, you will need one or more partners with similar appetites, compatible chemistry, and still more skill. Crew discord has torn asunder many a trip or, worse, endangered its participants.

It goes without saying that the expedition members should possess a high order of canoeing skills, but if you have a choice between good judgment and a good cross draw, go with the judgment. Although it is worthwhile to know *how* to run difficult rapids, it is essential to know *when not* to. There is an adage to the effect that "no Indian ever drowned on a portage." A wise crew weighs the objective elements of a given course, including water and air temperatures, time of day, and water levels, and also the subjective considerations of remoteness, the personality of the river, crew condition—both mental and physical—and the possible and probable consequences of a miscalculation.

Judgment is a product of experience. Having made progressively more difficult canoe trips, you and your crew should now have good canoeing and outdoor skills. In addition, longer and more remote travel calls for greater navigational ability, first-aid or medical training, and ingenuity in the selection of food, clothing, and gear. And physical conditioning in preparation for an expedition is paramount.

Generally, the most serious navigation challenges are the large lakes. The principles are no different from those described in chapter 9, but an experienced expeditioner is able to translate on a huge scale, even though unable to see the opposite shoreline or the extremity of an immense bay. Hugging a shoreline may be impractical, and calculated risks will be taken as the party strikes out across a broad reach of open water, bound for an almost indistinct headland. In the more northerly latitudes, the correct reading of the compass becomes quite difficult owing to magnetic variations from true north of 25 to 30 degrees and more in some areas (these variations are usually indicated in the map data).

EQUIPMENT

A carefully selected first-aid kit and basic first-aid knowledge on the part of at least one crew member is advisable. Knowing how to deal with hypothermia, heat stroke, severe bleeding, unconsciousness, or a broken bone is at a premium when an expedition is far from medical help.

Food selection and preparation in the bush becomes a high art when a crew embarks on a prolonged wilderness journey. Weight becomes a more critical consideration, as do the nutritive requirements for fueling a 25- to 40-mile-a-day regimen. A diet providing a balance of fats, carbohydrates, some protein, and roughage is essential to physical and mental well-being. Getting that balance is going to mean including some whole foods—cheeses, bacon, compressed meats or sausage—that add to the weight, but a diet exclusively of freeze-dried fare would bankrupt your crew, nutritionally and monetarily. Knowing how to make bannock bread on the trail is almost a necessity for an extended voyage. Fish may supplement the diet, but don't count on catching them in planning the menus.

We have outfitted parties of six for almost a month with what we could fit in our canoes and carry on our backs. For extended trips, or for other reasons, parties have sometimes arranged for air drops and caches at remote points.

In most of North America today it would be difficult, if not illegal, to attempt to live off the land. Much of the game is protected, and even if it were not, hunting is out of tune with the spirit of canoeing. We should be battling to preserve ever-dwindling wildlife resources. In that same vein, guns should not be a part of the canoe expeditioner's equipment, either for hunting or misguided ideas of protection. The actual cases of mauling or attacks by "wild" animals are statistically insignificant. They probably involved extraordinary circumstances and would have occurred no matter how well armed the victim. As far as bodily harm, more fatalities occur in one year as a result of bee stings than all the bear attacks ever recorded.

A clean campsite, with food well secured and positioned (please, not in the tent), out of the reach of bears, raccoons, and squirrels, will be the canoer's best protection against wildlife. If it is impractical to suspend food packs from a tree, put them under an overturned canoe, well anchored. A tarp or poncho stretched over the packs with rocks holding down the corners is also useful. One thing seems clear: The more remote the trip, the less likely it is that you will have unwanted visits from local wildlife. A remote wilderness campsite will not have had enough prior use to have become associated with food leavings, nor is it as likely to encroach on the animals' territory. Your most serious adversaries, by far, will be the mosquito and blackfly. Expeditioners will be wise to carry high-potency repellents and, in extreme conditions, head nets.

Most of the canoes, clothing, and gear suitable for canoe tripping will serve for an expedition, but with an even greater premium on quality and reliability. Take gear that will survive, along with whatever it takes to repair it. Canoes should be larger, and full-length decks (spray decks) are well worth considering. Depending on the waters contemplated, a spray deck provides warmth in addition to protection from rain and heavy standing waves.

FLY-IN LOGISTICS

Thorough research is your best safeguard against surprises. Use reliable maps and supplement them with firsthand accounts of prior expeditions, including those of early explorers. Corresponding or visiting with the members of earlier parties can clarify unclear or conflicting journal references; with luck, you can sit down with your source to mark your map with the locations of campsites, portages, dangerous obstacles, or points of interest. You will also want to know the weather and water levels prevailing during your informant's trip, in order to judge the relevance of descriptions of certain rapids or the location of portages (many routes have high- and low-water portages).

Getting to and from your points of access and egress (by definition, if it's easy, it's not an expedition) is going to be your greatest challenge and expense. In the Canadian wilds, we have employed cars, trains, float planes, wagons, and motor launches. Canoes have been shipped, often months beforehand, by truck, barge, float plane, and train, and sometimes, following the trip, they have had to winter on frozen wastes, until arrangements could be made to pick them up.

CANOES NORTH!

If your destination lies somewhere between 50 and 72 degrees north latitude, you're talking expedition. What does it take besides an imagination and a sense of adventure?

Paved highway and public transportation lead to some stupendous wilderness trips. Air travel, however has made it possible to get into and out of canoeing destinations that took 300 years of North American exploration to identify, much less explore. Flying is often the only practical way for canoe

Sometimes, the only way in—and out—is by float plane. Here, a Cessna 185 with a 17-foot, 80-pound expedition canoe lashed to pontoon struts. West Road River, British Columbia.

All the skills in the book are needed for running this wilderness river.

expeditioners to find their blue line, get out before ice-in, and make it back to Chicago to address their sales meeting.

The first leg is relatively easy—for the crew, at least. Scheduled air service is now available into a host of northern communities in the vast region above the 52nd parallel. These are the "gateway cities" into the north country: Bettles, Alaska; Dawson City and Whitehorse, Yukon Territories; Fort Simpson and Yellowknife, Northwest Territories; Lynn Lake, Saskatchewan; Churchill, Manitoba; and Schefferville, Quebec—just to mention a few. Your scheduled airline may fly a Pilatus Porter, a well-used DC-3, or a modern DC-10, but there is a timetable and you'll need reservations. I have yet to see a flight in this part of the world that wasn't booked to the gunwales.

Now you have to figure out how to get your canoes to the "gateway city" as well. Trucks are usually the answer, but make arrangements early to give the shipper lots of flexibility; meaning that he can haul when he's got plenty of room. That's also the way to negotiate a weight quotation rather than paying for volume or "cubes."

Getting the boats out at the end of the trip is even more difficult. We've used oil-field cargo planes, trains, trucks, and ocean tugs, and we've waited for up to a year before our boats reappeared. Also, Canadian customs can be a problem. Make sure that you can document the return of your boats to the United States.

The gateway cities all have something in common. You can find dining, accomodations, eskimo art, and charter air service, but all of them will cost you an arm and a leg. Get hold of the charter air service early in the planning process. Use the phone and then a letter to confirm. In addition to providing information on rates and logistics, the proprietor is a good source of information on your intended route. He will have looked at your rivers from the air, and knows the lay of the land. He may also be able to give you the name of other parties whom he has carried, and you may want to track down someone from that party. Aerial surveys, topos, and pilot observations are helpful, but there is no substitute for actual trip notes supplemented by talking with someone who has already done the trip.

Float plane service into the outback is not cheap, and the cost will depend on the type of aircraft available. The three most common are the Cessna 185 (or some similar suffix), the Beaver, and the Twin Otter. The smaller Cessnas may take one canoe on the floats, and two to three people and baggage. A Beaver may carry three to four persons, and two canoes on the struts. A Twin Otter can carry as many as six passengers, plus their gear, and two canoes on the outside. With luck, you may find a Twin Otter with an enlarged side door that can take six people and three canoes inside. You can expect to pay $2.00 to $2.50 a mile for the Cessna (Canadian), up to $3.50 a mile for a Beaver or single Otter, and up to $4.50 a mile for a Twin Otter. Canoes may or may not be an additional charge, and prices may rise or fall with the cost of fuel. Remember, you will also have to pay the mileage for an empty backhaul.

Be specific with the float plane operator about carrying canoes. Some may not be willing to carry more than one canoe on the outside. Talk to him about canoe length and overall weight (including the projected weight of your crew and baggage), and bring up the subject of emergency or contingency plans. The simplest plan, of course, is to have him fly a backtrack of your course if you are not at the agreed upon pickup spot at the appointed time.

Despite the time, hassle, and steep price, a plane charter is often the only practical way to fit a remote wilderness trip in with the demands of your other, more mundane life.

11

Competition

Competition canoeing in its many forms is growing rapidly in popularity but is still in its infancy. Until very recently, it has enjoyed greater status in Europe than in this country. This is particularly true for white-water events, inasmuch as Olympic flat-water paddling has been part of the U.S. scene for over fifty years. It is also ironic, considering the North American origins of the Eskimo kayak and the Indian canoe. However, this is all changing as more and more canoeists are trying their hand at the variety of competitive events open to them.

WHY COMPETE?

For many people, competition gives purpose to their sport by creating the need for training or simply showing them how they stack up. Whether your goal is physical fitness or ego gratification, there is no question that competition sharpens the senses and skills that will stand you in good stead in other phases of the sport. The slalom racer forced to turn where the gate is, rather than at will, is going to be a more proficient recreational boater, and the occasional marathon participant is

A pair of whitewater slalom competitors racing in the open, mixed (male and female), C-2 class.

173

not likely to be intimidated by a 30-mile day on a canoe trip.

For the canoer with serious aspirations, particularly in white-water competition, it is an "open" sport, requiring no club affiliation, and without an intricate maze of "seeding" or qualifying criteria. All that's required is a boat, paddles, and a partner. Increasingly, however, the weekend paddler and some-time racer is being superseded by the full-time disciplined specialist.

There is a bewildering array of canoeing and kayaking competitions reflecting the diversity of the sport, the boats, and regional preferences. Marathon flatwater racing is most popular in the midwest and northeast; whitewater racing in both decked and open canoes is most popular in the northeast and southeast; outrigger canoe racing is becoming popular in California; and in Hawaii, almost every town worthy of the name supports an outrigger canoe club. Triathlons which include canoeing, biking and running have been around for over 25 years and seem to have the broadest attraction for the citizen or recreational racer. If none of these appeal to you, try canoe poling, dead fish polo (a major European sport, with Olympic aspirations), or canoe orienteering. Let's look at the more popular of the canoeing competitions.

BOAT CLASSIFICATIONS

The sport of "canoeing" actually embraces both kayaks and canoes. In fact, Europeans, when they use the term canoeing, are likely to be referring to kayaking, and a majority of the boats competing under the auspices of the International Canoe Federation are also kayaks. Put simply, the sport is canoeing; the boats come in different shapes and sizes.

Olympic flatwater boats—both canoes and kayaks—are a different breed, looking more like racing shells and demanding specialized paddling techniques. The boats likely to be seen in your local or international whitewater events will be organized, announced, and reported as K-1, K-1W (men's and women's solo kayak, and C-1, C-2, C-1W, C-2W, C-2M (single and double canoes for men, women, and mixed. The prefix "O" is added for "open", so that OC-2M designates an open, two-place canoe, paddled by a man and a woman.

Within the international flatwater and whitewater classes and the broader classifications sanctioned by the American Canoe Association (ACA), there are continually evolving specifications meant to define and limit the designs of particular boats for particular events, such as width, length, some dimension ratios, etc. The aim, generally, is to limit the proliferation of boats, classes, events, and formats without stifling diversity. The goal always sought, seldom

Five-time World-Champion C-1 paddler
Jon Lugbill.

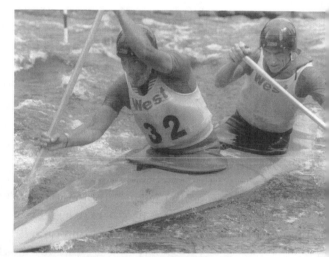

Slalom C-2 competitors
Don Sorenson and Ray McLean.

achieved, is to match like-hull against like-hull, and like-contestant against like-contestant. As with most sports, the health of canoe racing depends on broad based participation by "citizen racers." Thus, race directors invariably create separate divisions for recreational hulls (and paddlers). Most family tripping canoes, no matter how strong the paddlers, are no match for an 18 1/2-foot, straight keeled, 40-pound canoe with a 32-inch width at the 4-inch waterline. For both flatwater and whitewater racing, there is usually some combination of weight and hull dimension restrictions that keeps competitors on a level playing field.

TYPES OF COMPETITION

Olympic Flatwater Competition

A team from Washington, D.C., represented the United States in its Olympic canoeing debut at the 1924 Paris Games. In recent years, paddlers from the United States have done well in Olympic competition. Greg Barton was a double gold medalist in Seoul (in K-2 with Norm Bellingham in), and we have a new crop of medal candidates for the 1996 games in Atlanta. Races are on flatwater for sprint distances of 500 and 1,000 meters, and a long distance of 10,000 meters (6.2 miles). The boats are K-1, K-2, K-4, both men and women, and C-1 and C-2, men only. Olympic Flatwater canoes and kayaks are V-bottomed hulls, requiring lots of boat time and well developed skills, but nothing goes faster under paddle and they are magnificent to watch.

Whitewater Competition

For both open and closed boats the races are of two types: slalom and downriver (sometimes called "wildwater" in closed boat races). The most popular international sport is in decked (closed) canoes and kayaks. Kayaks (K-1) are raced by both men and women, and canoes (C-1 and C-2), by men or mixed. Today's slalom canoes are almost indistinguishable from kayaks: wafer thin and eggshell light, except that the paddler kneels and uses a single-bladed paddle. The United States has consistently produced some of the best slalom canoe paddlers in the world: Jon Lugbill and David Hearn both have been World Champion many times; Scott Strasbough and Joe Jacobi won a gold medal in C-2 at the Olympics in Barcelona in 1992.

Slalom competitors negotiate 25 gates over a distance of 800 meters, usually Class III (80 percent of the course) and Class IV water, and are scored on both elapsed time and penalties for missed gates and "touches." Downriver races involve no gates and are run point-to-point over at least three kilometers and usually six to 12 kilometers on Class I to II water (international caliber wildwater races might contain Class III and IV water). Slalom racing in decked boats is the international sport—and an Olympic event in 1992 and 1996—but in North America there is increasing interest in open canoe, whitewater racing. The format is much the same as for the decked boats, with obvious adjustments made for the larger, less maneuverable open canoes—but not much! In recent years, radical designs, eggshell-thin hulls, and special outfitting have made the open whitewater canoes almost as agile as their decked counterparts.

Marathon Racing

Perhaps a misnomer, a canoe "marathon" covers no standard distance; distances for most races are in the five to 10 mile range, with long courses of 20 to 30 miles, and ultras which can be up to a hundred or several hundred miles and several days in duration. Marathon racing is generally done on flatwater, seldom more challenging than Class I. Races are usually conducted under the rules of the United States Canoe Association (USCA) and the American Canoe Association (ACA). The former has developed standards especially related to classes and hulls.

Despite the grueling connotation of its name, marathon racing is the sport that will be most attractive to recreational and social racers. Most races are organized to attract the citizen racer, with many classes geared towards recreational hulls. Race site requirements are obviously not as rigorous as with whitewater events; any pond, lake, canal or impoundment will do; in fact, waterways suitable for little else will make for adequate marathon-style racing.

Marathon racing at the advanced level involves equipment, skills, training regimens, racing strategies and athletes equivalent to those found in bicycle or cross-country ski racing (sports in which many of the top paddlers also participate). Racers compete in C-1 and C-2, both men's and women's classes. Larger races will offer classes for juniors (16 and under), junior/senior (one paddler over 35 and the other, under 16), mixed (man and woman), and masters (over 40). At championship meets held over several days, it is not unusual for paddlers to compete in three or four events, perhaps a C-1 event, senior men's team, and paired with a woman in mixed C-2.

The advanced racers paddle canoes that fall into two main categories: competition cruisers and pro boats, otherwise known as 432 or 327 hulls; the first indicating a 32-inch width at the four-inch waterline, the latter, a 27-inch

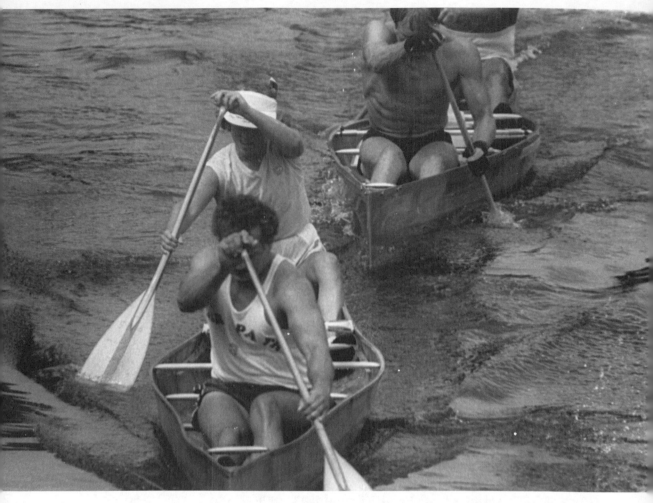

Pro boats compete in marathon races of 5- to 25-mile distances, with some ultra-distance races considerably longer and a few that extend for several days. Top racers may reach stroke cadences of 70 strokes per minute. Here, the trailing boat is "wake riding" on the lead boat: akin to "drafting" on a bicycle.

width at the 3-inch waterline. These boats are usually Kevlar or woodstrip and weigh about 35 pounds. The solo C-1s will weigh about 25 pounds. The pro boats and fastest C-1s are designed to tweak the USCA hull limitations, and require well-tuned paddling skills. The competition cruiser class is a more forgiving hull, efficient and quick, but stable and commodious enough to be drafted into service as a weekend family tripper.

Beyond the Marathon

One of the most popular sports of the eighties has been the triathlon, consisting in its most popular form of swimming, cycling and running. The original triathlons had paddling as the waterborne segment: canoes, kayaks and Australian surf skis. From coast-to-coast are creative variations, with up to five events, some lasting for days. Almost all of these multi-sport events emphasize relay formats as well as "Ironman" classes. Relays encourage many weekend athletes to grab a few buddies and join in the fun. I judge the events by the scenery, the course layout, number of aid stations, and the quality of the post-race party and music; the intensity of the competition is important, but secondary, to many of us.

And All The Rest

In addition to the racing categories already described, there are a number of events that merit attention. Canoe poling, which at one time was considered a necessary adjunct to whitewater running and expedition canoeing, has few practitioners today. The "setting pole" and techniques for climbing a river or "snubbing" (letting down a rapid), have perhaps given way to better paddling techniques and tougher canoes. More roads leading to upstream put-ins and a deficiency of Maine guides to teach canoe poling may also have contributed to the demise of the skill. Poling has, however, been revived in the form of a competitive activity by a growing band of dedicated practitioners. Since 1975, national poling championships sanctioned by the ACA have permitted competitors to test their agility, speed, endurance, and water-reading skills. Using lightweight aluminum poles and perfected techniques, they can perform feats of upstream and downstream travel that the old-timers would admire, and which would put a mere paddler to shame. Since old-time Maine-type guides are practically nonexistent, especially outside of Maine, the aspiring canoe poler may have to do a little research to find either a pole or an instructor. A local canoe club affiliated with the ACA is probably the best place to start.

Dead fish polo is an adaptation of kayak polo, a very popular and competitive sport in Great Britain and continental Europe. Within a conscribed area of flatwater, paddlers in teams use boat and paddles to move the "dead fish" to the goal. The derivative game played in open canoes by solo or tandem paddlers, may involve getting the dead fish (a sponge) into the other guy's boat and winning points for humiliation. The game can be used to increase boat handling skills, since the players are forced to be extraordinarily inventive in their strokes in order to survive.

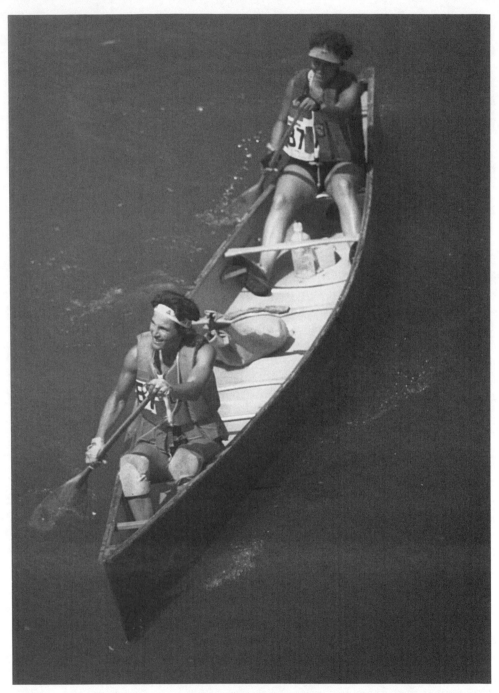

These recreational racers are on the 25-mile canoeing leg of the Ski to Sea race, an all-day relay composed of six events—not including the post-race party!

Map and compass skills, route finding and canoe racing are combined in canoe orienteering, known among its practitioners as Canoe-O. This sport is simply an adaptation of the popular land-based sport, in which competitors find their way from point A to point B, by way of intermediate control or checkpoints, and finish order is determined by elapsed time. An orienteer might have to choose between the 2-mile winding road or ¾-mile bushwack through the ravine to reach an objective. For the canoe orienteer, the question may be, should he paddle the ox-bow or portage the isthmus? A course might range from five to 15 miles in length, and, like marathon racing, there are distinctions made between recreational and serious competitors.

Almost any of the competitive canoeing events described in this chapter can be pursued to an elite level, with competitions occurring both nationally and internationally. For most of us, however, these events are just "games" for the off-season—the times when we can't be off on a two-week canoe trip. Aside from the excitement of the competitions themselves, all of them contribute greatly to our skills.

12

Motorized Canoes

Canoeing is best enjoyed as a self-propelled sport, but to entirely shun the motor is to deny the versatility of the canoe. The motor's noise and smell may be an unnatural match for the canoe, but there are times when a marriage of convenience can be the answer to a special need. Despite the weight of motor and gas (five gallons weighs almost 25 pounds), which might slow you down on a portage, a 2½ hp motor can be a veritable lake eater, enabling you to cover three to four times the distance possible with paddles alone.

The motor might be accessory to a trip whose primary focus was fishing or photography, and where the time required to reach a distant target did not permit the leisure of paddling. It could be used by a large family group to reach a base camp beyond the crowded, close-in waters; after which the canoers could resort to self-propulsion for making their daily forays to fish, photograph, or explore. For a trip intended to be primarily by paddle, one motor can be used to tow the entire party (we have towed as many as five fully loaded canoes using one 2½ hp outboard) up a large, heavily trafficked lake, to put both lake and people behind us before commencing on the canoe trip proper. Finally, an entire canoe trip with two or

183

Towing canoes behind a motor launch may give your canoe trip a head start.

three canoes could employ the services of one small outboard (and provision for towing) to make an extended trip, difficult by paddle alone.

The motor should not be a substitute for paddles, but it can save many miles of head-down slogging and allow the freedom to paddle and explore those stretches of water that appeal to the trippers. Motorized canoeing is definitely not a way to beat wind and waves. Against a moderate headwind the motor is a boon, but when whitecaps appear, head for shore, either to determine a strategy employing paddles or patiently sit it out. The relentless push of the motor on rough water is no substitute for two paddlers riding with the waves, adjusting their strokes and body action to the seas beneath them. In short, if you can't paddle it, don't motor it.

The Motor Mount

There are square-ended canoes obviously designed to take a motor. Less obvious is the fact that a motor squeezed onto the narrow end of such a canoe, with its handle poking into the small of the stern rider's back, is an awkward arrangement, to say the least. Preferable is a standard canoe using a well-designed motor mount which puts motor and handle alongside the person in the stern, eliminating the need to twist around or grope for a handle behind you. The compromise is, of course, that the motor offset to one side is going to require counterbalancing by positioning both packs and paddlers for proper trim.

There are commercially available motor mounts that are adaptable to all canoe models. Look for an adjustable one that can be clamped securely to the

A small motor mounted to the side of the stern seat is an effective lake eater.

A tow harness using a giant bowline around the hull and a paddle for quick release prevents "hogging" by the towed canoe.

gunwale with a minimum of fuss. A hardwood or marine-plywood mounting block completes the requirements.

Size

Small electric motors are extremely light and quiet, but the battery pack is heavy and cumbersome if any portaging is required. A small gas outboard of less than 5 hp is the best bet. Find a gas can of undoubted integrity too; despite deft handling, gasoline and its fumes have a way of permeating everything within seventeen feet of it. Many engines require a gas-oil mixture, so be sure you know the proportions before you get into the bush, and make sure the gas is kept free of dirt and sand and filtered for good measure. A screwdriver, small wrench, plenty of shear pins, and crossed fingers should prepare you for the inevitable snags and rocks.

Towing

If two or more canoes are involved, you will need a good towing harness. Do not attempt to tow using the normal bow and stern rings on the canoe since this will cause the following canoe to "hog," or swing back and forth in whiplike fashion. Instead, make a giant loop with a bowline knot and slide it over the bow of the canoe, positioning the knot directly under the keel line. If the canoe to be towed is loaded, the weight should be slightly toward the stern, which will also help the canoe to plane rather than hog. Inserting the paddle blade through your giant bowline and under the front seat or thwart holds the loop in place and allows for quick dismantlement, in an emergency or otherwise. If you are going to be towing your own party, the passengers can be in their normal positions in the following canoes with the stern paddlers on the alert, using paddles as occasional rudders to maintain alignment.

Portaging

If you are going to be facing some portages, take along a pack frame to which you can fasten motor, mount, and gas can to carry across as a separate load. Do not attempt to portage the canoe with the mount still attached, since it will tend to grab every passing bush, and those few pounds at the end of the canoe are the equivalent of twenty additional pounds square on your back. Likewise, trying to carry motor and gas can like suitcases is awkward and tiring for all but the shortest portages.

It is worth repeating that you should not attempt to motor on water you would not paddle, nor should you plan a canoe trip around a motor. Canoers should choose the trip and determine the utility of the motor after all the imponderables and variables have been considered. I would also be hesitant to take a trip where I had to rely on a motor to get me there and back, inasmuch as modern inventions have a way of breaking down at inopportune moments; in other words, the total mileage should always be a distance that could be paddled, even if at a considerable cost in time and physical effort.

Afterword

A Plea for the Waterways

In 1974, Americans experienced for the first time a shortage in a commodity they had come to take for granted—had, in fact, come to depend on—oil. We have also taken for granted another and far more priceless asset—our water resources. Industrialization, power, irrigation, flood control, harvests, mineral extraction, land development, population pressure—all wage a relentless battle against our waterways, and the waterways are losing.

The analogy with oil is all too valid. We have never set a proper value on our water resources and have squandered them accordingly. It is not uncommon to discover that, from time to time, certain of our rivers have had 110 percent of their annual average flow allocated to various users. Often the worthy purpose is irrigation, so that farming is encouraged on arid land where only the availability of cheap water makes agriculture possible.

The natural and perennial flooding of certain rivers provides the excuse for politicians to promote still more pork-barrel dam-building projects rather than pursue undramatic flood-plain zoning. An entire bureaucracy is kept busy looking for new dam sites. In the name of flood control,

187

power, and recreation (usually meaning motorboats), dams and their associated impoundments are built. The result is that only a handful of rivers are left in the United States where one can travel for more than a few days without encountering some man-made obstruction; fewer still, where the traveler will find some semblance of the primitive state. Unfortunately, much of the work of man is irreversible.

In 1967—and none too soon—the Wild and Scenic Rivers Act was passed by Congress, designating twenty-seven candidates for possible inclusion and setting a ten-year schedule for determining which rivers would qualify. The process is agonizingly slow. Studies are not begun until several years after they are authorized, and then it takes as long as four or five years to complete a report. Nevertheless, progress has been made, and the national system now includes about 2,300 miles on 28 stretches of river, with 841 miles classified as wild, 774 as scenic, and 702 as recreational. These classifications are defined as follows:

Wild: Unpolluted, undammed, and primitive surroundings accessible only by trails

Scenic: Undammed, with shoreline largely undeveloped, accessible by road

Recreational: Readily accessible, with some development and pre-existing dams allowed

Despite this progress, the number of protected waterways is minimal compared to those irretrievably lost through years of neglect and exploitation. At the same time, river use by canoers, kayakers, and rafters (both commercial and private) is escalating at a phenomenal rate. In the period 1970 to 1976, the number of rafters, canoeists, and kayakers on the Youghiogheny in Pennsylvania leaped from 17,000 to 95,500. Here, and on the Potomac in Maryland, boaters must literally queue up to gain access to the river or enter a rapid.

On popular western rivers, such as the Colorado, the Rogue and the Salmon, one must have a permit to run, and a battle rages between commercial rafters, who have the lion's share of the permit allocations, and private boaters, who sometimes must wait years to run them.

Rafting, particularly as it has escalated to its most rapacious commercial forms, has given hundreds of thousands of curious, well-heeled adventurers a taste of white-water excitement, but they are missing the essential element of intimacy. Unlike solitary and tandem canoeists, who must deal with every whim and truculence of a busily descending river and who live by the fruits or penalties of their execution, rafters are more of a tour group who have placed themselves in the hands of a tour director.

Our waterways are a scarce resource which requires protection.

In the popular canoe-tripping areas, the influx of enthusiastic but environmentally thoughtless legions of canoers has created sanitation, litter, and waterway degradation problems. Too late, we have discovered how little remains to be enjoyed in a semi-wild or pristine state. Then, too, many have rushed to take to the waters and the trails before fully understanding the safe and sane pursuit of the sport, and often without an appreciation or knowledge of living in nondestructive harmony with the wilderness environment. In this sense, at least, the permit system—where it exists—has been the savior of certain waterways. Strict regulation has meant that one can pull into camp on the Middle Fork of the Salmon, for example, and be scarcely aware that a dozen people camped on that same site the previous night, and perhaps every night for the past two weeks.

As discouraging as this may sound, the situation is far from hopeless. And there are certainly many thousands of miles of water where the canoeist can enjoy solitude, history, and scenic beauty—if not untamed wilderness. But the battle must be fought vigorously on the political front by a growing constituency of paddlers who would preserve as much of what remains as possible, and endeavor, as well, to reclaim whatever may be salvageable. Our water resources, and the vast network of lakes and rivers upon which our country grew and was nurtured, is worth preserving—for those who paddle today and for our children and grandchildren, who should not be denied this priceless part of our North American heritage.